FOUNDATIONS
°F
MAGIC

About the Author

J. F. O'Neill's pursuit of magical knowledge and skills has paralleled his career in psychology as a hypnotherapist, counselor, and seminar leader. He studied Gestalt Therapy with Bethal Pahaigh and once ran a private practice in Neuro-Linguistic Programming (NLP).

To Write to the Author

If you wish to contact the author or would like more information about this book, please write to the author in care of Llewellyn Worldwide and we will forward your request. Both the author and publisher appreciate hearing from you and learning of your enjoyment of this book and how it has helped you. Llewellyn Worldwide cannot guarantee that every letter written to the author can be answered, but all will be forwarded. Please write to:

J. F. O'Neill
℅ Llewellyn Worldwide
P.O. Box 64383, Dept. 0-7387-0743-0
St. Paul, MN 55164-0383, U.S.A.
Please enclose a self-addressed stamped envelope for reply,
or $1.00 to cover costs. If outside U.S.A., enclose
international postal reply coupon.

Many of Llewellyn's authors have websites with additional information and resources. For more information, please visit our website at:
http://www.llewellyn.com

FOUNDATIONS
ᵒF
MAGIC

TECHNIQUES
& SPELLS
THAT WORK

J. F. O'NEILL

Llewellyn Publications
St. Paul, Minnesota

First Edition
First Printing, 2005

Book design and layout by Joanna Willis
Cover design by Kevin R. Brown
Cover images © 2004 by Brand X Pictures, PhotoDisc

Llewellyn is a registered trademark of Llewellyn Worldwide, Ltd.

Library of Congress Cataloging-in-Publication Data
O'Neill, J. F., 1944 –
    Foundations of magic : techniques & spells that work / J. F. O'Neill.
      p. cm.
    Includes index.
    ISBN 0-7387-0743-0
    1. Magic I. Title.
    BF1611.O54 2005
    133.4'3—dc22   2005045165

Llewellyn Worldwide does not participate in, endorse, or have any authority or responsibility concerning private business transactions between our authors and the public.
   All mail addressed to the author is forwarded but the publisher cannot, unless specifically instructed by the author, give out an address or phone number.
   Any Internet references contained in this work are current at publication time, but the publisher cannot guarantee that a specific location will continue to be maintained. Please refer to the publisher's website for links to authors' websites and other sources.

Llewellyn Publications
A Division of Llewellyn Worldwide, Ltd.
P.O. Box 64383, Dept. 0-7387-0743-0
St. Paul, MN 55164-0383, U.S.A.
www.llewellyn.com

Printed in the United States of America

Dedicated to Mary Catherine

My friend, partner, wife, and really mean editor,
who took away so many of my very precious words

CONTENTS

List of Exercises   xi
Acknowledgments   xii

PART I – A COURSE IN SPELLCRAFT

Introduction 3

How to Use This Book 7

1   **Magic** 11

    Magic Defined 11

    Magic *Not* to Be Found in *Foundations of Magic* 13

    Old Magic and New Magic 13

    White and Black Magic 14

    High and Low Magic 14

    Magic and Power 14

    Magic and Science 15

    Magic and Religion 15

    Believing in Magic 16

    Ritual and Ceremony 17

    Words of Power 19

    The Astral Plane and Astral Travel 20

    Your True Nature or Higher Self 20

Theory vs. Practice 21
Some Problems with Success 22
Magical Symbols, Substances, and Implements 23
Some Laws of Magic 23

2 The Psychology of Magic 27
The Law of Pretending 28
The Unconscious Mind 31
The Conscious Mind 32
Conscious-Unconscious Mind Agreement .33
Problems, Unconscious Parts, and Benefits 33
Thoughts and Feelings 37
Participants, Observers, and Memories 42
Intention, Incubation, and Letting Go 47
Humor 51
Hypnotic Trance 52
Self-Hypnosis 53
Higher States 59

3 Casting Spells 63
The Preparation Stages 63
Designing a Well-Formed Intention 64
Rehearsal 71
Self-Preparation 71
Physical Preparations 72
Ritual 75
Follow-up 81
When a Spell Doesn't Seem to Work 84
Ethics 87
About the Format in Part II 88
Be Prudent 89

PART II – THE SPELLS

Attracting Someone for Fun and Lust 93

Attracting the Right Love Partner 96

Finding Love 102

Spell for an Unfaithful Lover 106

Help in Parenting 110

Healing an Injury 114

Alleviating Chronic Pain 118

Alleviating Acute Pain 122

Transforming Chronic or Serious Illness 126

Eliminating an Allergy 131

Attracting Money, Short-Term 135

Attracting Money, Long-Term 138

Improving Your Business or Career 143

Luck at Gambling 148

Realizing Self-Esteem 151

Increasing Personal Power 157

Resolving Persistent Problems 160

Finding a Lost Item 164

Not Taking Yourself or Your Situation so Seriously 166

Resolving Uncomfortable Situations 169

Changing Your Self-Image 174

Eliminating Depression or the Blues 179

Eliminating a Phobia 183

Increasing Your Confidence 188

A Binding Spell 192

Getting Rid of Pests 195

Achieving a Willed Purpose 198

Helping Another Person Achieve a Willed Purpose 201

Making a Difficult Decision 206

Helping Your Distressed Plant or Animal 211

Bringing Out the Sun 214

Bringing the Rain 216

Stopping Someone Who Talks Too Much 219

APPENDICES

1. *Achieving Altered States: A Summary Outline* 225

2. *Designing a Well-Formed Intention: A Summary Outline* 229

3. *The Steps in Casting a Spell: A Summary Outline* 231

4. *The Practice Spell of Chapter 3* 235

5. *How to Make an Incense Burner* 239

6. *Making a Talisman Using Magic Squares* 241

Index 245

EXERCISES

1. Appreciating Your Problems 37
2. Becoming Familiar with Modes of Thinking and Feeling 39
3. Do You Remember Events as a Participant or an Observer? 43
4. Experiencing Feelings in a Memory 44
5. Creating and Experiencing an Artificial Memory 46
6. Practicing Self-Hypnosis 58
7. Practice Ascending to a Higher State 61
8. A Practice Spell 81

ACKNOWLEDGMENTS

My thanks to Eveline van Ginkel and Elenor Quirk for their valuable suggestions and for the time she took correcting mistakes in the original manuscript. Of the many magicians who have influenced my life, I particularly wish to acknowledge John Grinder, Michael Hartley, Bethal Phaigh, and Yanina Sloman.

Part I

A COURSE IN SPELLCRAFT

INTRODUCTION

M y guiding principle when writing *Foundations of Magic* was to create a primer for the art and craft of casting spells. The subject of spellcraft or practical magic is vast, however, and the time required to become adept at it can be considerable. Nonetheless I desired an approach that would yield dependable success from reading a single, modest volume demanding only a moderate investment of time. To accomplish this, I have limited background material and instruction to just the essential knowledge and specific skills required to cast the particular thirty-three spells contained between these covers.

I have also eliminated almost all attempts at explanation of why magic works. Besides fostering confusion, the bewildering range of models and belief systems used to explain magic can discourage the most enthusiastic seeker. Contradiction and inconsistency abound, and while most people sense a core of basic truths, the competing ideas and beliefs seem to demand either outright rejection of the whole enterprise or else blind commitment to one school. Attempts at scientific explanation only add to the problem as they are inevitably some rehash of an old explanation dressed in ill-fitting scientific garb. They are always decidedly unscientific and only detract from the legitimacy so longingly sought.

I have attempted to minimize the burden of explanation and the difficulties arising from conflicting schools of thought in four ways: description, direct experience, secularism, and minimizing jargon. Allow me elaborate on these one at a time.

Description

By relying on description, I have attempted to circumvent the issue of explanation as much as possible. Most descriptions of magical power, including those elicited in casting a spell, have three things in common, and to my mind these constitute the essence of what is important:

1. Magical forces can effect changes in individuals and the world around them.

2. Magical forces manifest and can be directed, by an act of focused will on the part of an individual (or individuals) who has undertaken adequate preparation and performed appropriate actions or rituals.

3. Magical forces operate through different mechanisms than, and lie outside of, the realm of normal or mundane psychological and physical phenomena.[1]

Some people feel that without an explanation for a phenomenon they cannot fully understand it. In most cases I believe this is a mistaken notion. Take, for instance, a bird. If for some bizarre reason, you had never encountered a bird and wanted to understand what it was, would you rather have a bird explained or would you rather have a bird *described* to you? Explanations answer "why" and descriptions answer "what" (and procedural descriptions answer "how"). For practical understanding, explanations are usually one of the least valuable types of information, and descriptions one of the most valuable.

Direct Experience

Consider how much more meaningful, even than a description, a direct encounter would be in your quest to understand a bird. You could see it, watch it fly, hear the sounds it makes, and with enough exposure, you would have a pretty good understanding of what a bird is—or at least that type of bird. The same applies to your understanding of magic; a fact that will be underscored in chapters 2 and 3 with a number of learning exercises. These exercises will allow you to directly experience the application of various concepts discussed in Part I of this book. Direct experience is

---

1. As will be discussed in chapter 1, although different in their source and nature, magical forces must work in harmony with the other laws of nature.

also fundamental to the various preparation stages of each spell. To read the preparation instructions without actually doing them would be fruitless, for it is what you experience that prepares you.

Secularism

Foundations of Magic is secular in the sense that it does not explicitly emphasize any school of magic, and it does not require you to adopt any specific belief system. It uses as its basis the essence of magic free of any supporting dogma. For those whom this book is their initial introduction to practical magic, and choose to pursue their studies in the craft, they can move on relatively unburdened with the defining explanations of any specific tradition. Those who are already experienced in the ancient art can incorporate the material in this book into their particular practice with little interference with what they already hold to be true.

Minimizing Jargon

A natural part of following a tradition or mastering a skill is learning the specialized vocabulary that accompanies it. This of course is true for the various schools of magic. For example, students who incorporate elements of the Qabala into their practice talk about the ten Sefiroth which are qualities of God's divine emanations. Followers of the tradition of the Order of the Golden Dawn refer to an idealized "middle pillar," a strived-for direction toward spiritual development. Jargon of this type can be very useful as it allows colleagues working an a specialized discipline to communicate more easily with one another about concepts and fine distinctions particular to their field or tradition.

Nevertheless, there can be detrimental aspects to jargon and primary among them is the tendency to mystify a subject. There is, of course, a great deal of mystery inherent in the practice of magic, which to many constitutes part of its allure; but mystery and mystification are usually antithetical to promoting understanding and providing clear instructions for a new skill set. Plain, concise language is what is desired here. There is another reason to minimize the use of jargon. Although there is some crossover, to varying degrees different magical traditions use a different vernacular to describe the same things. Even more confusing, the same words are often used to among the various schools to indicate slightly different meanings.

The degree to which I have succeeded in creating a work that allows one to quickly begin practicing effective, practical magic will ultimately have to be judged by you, the reader now scanning these lines. Nevertheless, I am gratified that my goal has in great measure been met. I base this assessment on feedback from those many people who have read a version of this manuscript in its various incarnations, and on the results I have witnessed by those who have practiced its methods in workshops both in North America and Europe.

To my delight, *Foundations of Magic* has also emerged as a solid resource for those already adept at the ancient art. What makes this book useful for the experienced practitioner of spellcraft, as well as the initiate, is the detailed information and instructions on psychological methods of self-preparation and altered states required for effectively casting a spell—especially those methods from cutting-edge psychological models such as Neuro-Linguistic Programming (NLP) and Ericksonian techniques. The connection between psychology and magic may not be obvious, but it is not new; the two have always been inseparable. Much of what we would consider as belonging firmly in the realm of psychological knowledge and practice was in past times thought of as an integral part of the magical arts.

J. F. O'Neill
June 2005

HOW TO USE
THIS BOOK

W elcome. You are about to enter the world of magic. Your keys to entry are an understanding of how to use this book and careful attention to what is written in it. The door to this world will not open freely if either key is ignored.

Foundations of Magic is divided into two parts: Part I comprises a brief course on spellcraft. Attempts have been made to limit the material in Part I only to what is relevant to this purpose and every effort has been made to keep the writing clear and concise. You will need to be thoroughly familiar with the material in Part I before moving on to Part II.

Part II consists of an individual set of detailed instructions for each spell. Each set of instructions is presented in a standard format designed to facilitate familiarity and ease of following along while casting a spell. This is thoroughly explained in the *Rehearsal* section of chapter 3. The instructions also include cross-references to relevant sections in Part I and the appendices. The appendices contain reference materials that are useful as summary guides or instructions for some of the procedures and practices discussed in both Parts I and II.

Despite whatever your first impression might be, the contents and organization of *Foundations of Magic* is not difficult or complex. On the contrary, if you follow the simple instructions outlined below, you will soon realize that the material in this volume has been written and laid out in a clear, straightforward manner. If you are conscientious in following these instructions, you can be using *Foundations of Magic* to cast effective, powerful spells in just a few days. **Under no circumstances attempt to work any spells without following and completing the instructions below.**

1. Carefully read the three chapters of Part I. Be sure you understand the concepts and procedures that are discussed.

2. Be diligent about completing all of the exercises in chapters 2 and 3.

3. When you have completed steps 1 and 2, you are ready to work any of the thirty-three spells. Choose a spell and follow the instructions in Part II thoroughly and carefully. Complete all of the preparations and practice the procedures until you are confident that you can enact them smoothly and from memory. **Do not vary any of the procedures for the Preparation or the Ritual.**

4. Perform the ritual of casting the spell.

Once steps 1 and 2 are completed, they obviously need not be repeated for each spell, although periodic review can be helpful.

At various points throughout this book, certain common words and phrases are used to convey very specific meanings. For instance, in chapter 2 the words *participant* and *observer* are employed to describe two distinctly different perspectives from which to experience a memory, daydream, or fantasy. Such designated words are printed in italics whenever they are used to convey these specific meanings. Where their general usage is intended they are not italicized.

To solve the problem of which pronouns to use in order to avoid gender-biased language, a convention has been chosen which is sure to upset those who are offended by violations of conventional normative grammar. Instead of the awkwardness of endless repetitions of "he or she," or the sometimes equally jarring balanced distribution of "he" and "she" throughout the text, plural pronouns are used. "They," "them," and "their" are used where, in the past, "he," "him," or "his" would have been used to denote a person of unspecified sex. The only justification offered for this grammatical heresy is the fact that such usage is becoming increasingly common in spoken English.

Scattered throughout the text of this book are instructions regarding which hand to use—right or left—for specific exercises or procedures. These instructions are intended for right-handed people. If you are left-handed and following these instructions proves awkward, feel free to switch hands.

1

MAGIC

The magic embodied in *Foundations of Magic* derives from established traditions of Western ritual or ceremonial magic, and contains elements from Hermetic, Wiccan, and Qabalistic practices.[1] Its roots are ancient. It is magic that, when competently practiced, is extremely powerful. It is magic that allows you to accomplish legitimate goals and make appropriate changes, both for yourself and, if care is taken, for others. Reading through the list of spells in the table of contents gives you a good idea of the range of things that can be accomplished, from the simple and mundane (such as finding a lost set of keys) to the profound (such as increasing personal power). There is no aspect of your life that cannot be greatly improved through the proper use of these spells.

Magic Defined

What is magic? A good starting point from which to answer this question is the simple but incomplete definition of magic formulated by Aleister Crowley. Crowley was

---

1. The Qabala refers to a set of systems and symbols of magic and mysticism that has its origins in ancient Judaism. Over the centuries it has undergone many transformations under the influences of cultures and religions including those of Gnosticism, Neoplatonism, Christianity, and Hermetic magic. There are a number of different English spellings in common use including Kabbalah, Cabala, Cabbalah, and Qubalah. Some authorities use specific spellings to indicate different Qabalistic traditions. Qabala is used throughout this book without regard to distinctions of origin or practice.

a colorful magician of the early twentieth century who possessed a strong personality and, in the minds of many, a disreputable character.[2] He described magic as *"the Science and Art of causing change to occur in conformity with Will."* This would seem to imply that any intentional act that achieved its purpose, such as taking out the garbage, was magic. Although in a limited way this is true, this is not what Crowley meant, as he had a special meaning in mind when he used the word *"Will."* *Will*, as Crowley often used it and as it is used here, is *intention* that is in complete concert with an individual's essential or *true nature.*[3] A person's *true nature* refers to one's nature free of the distortions or internal conflicts caused by beliefs, ego, personality, culture and the other psychological and psychic adornments that we all take on in order to survive in the world. This type of human *Will* is very powerful and is much more than just a psychological component of a person's makeup. It constitutes a form of energy that can directly influence events in the world. It is not only the vehicle for **intending** the changes that result from magic but also a vehicle for **effecting** those changes. A more precise reworking of Crowley's definition, and the one that is operational in this book is:

Magic is the Art and Craft of using Will as the agent for causing desired changes to occur.

The remainder of this chapter is a series of brief discussions on various topics and concepts of magic. Knowledge of these concepts will be useful, and in some cases essential, for the effective working of spells. We begin with a short survey of what the magic embraced in *Foundations of Magic* is *not*.

---

2. Any serious student of Western magic will repeatedly encounter Crowley. He was prolific, producing countless books and journal articles. He engendered strong feelings and opinions in others and discussions of his ideas, methods, and lifestyle are common in the literature. What does seem clear about Aleister Crowley is that he engaged in some areas of magic that are potentially dangerous and of questionable virtue. Anyone but an experienced practitioner of magic would be well advised to approach his teachings with caution.

3. Throughout *Foundations of Magic,* the word *Will* is capitalized when used with this meaning.

Magic *Not* to Be Found in *Foundations of Magic*

This magic is not stage magic, and you will not learn to saw people in half or to materialize poultry from inside a hat, or engage in any other entertaining form of perceptual illusion. This magic has nothing to do with invoking or evoking spirits (theurgy), communicating with the deceased (necromancy), demonology, satanism, or sacrifices. It does not give you power over other people in the sense that you can force them to act against their will. It does not provide you with a means to curse people, take revenge, or to advance your own interests at the expense of others. It will not allow you to achieve things that are not consistent with your own human nature (for instance, flying without the aid of an aircraft or walking through walls without the aid of a door).

Old Magic and New Magic

There is a common idea that the more ancient the magic, the more authentic and powerful it is. It is true that some of the magi of past ages were formidable and are reported to have accomplished miraculous feats. It does not necessarily follow, however, that the same magicians using the same practices would have the same results today. Different cultures and different ages require different actions in order to be effective in any arena of endeavor, and magic is no exception. Any student of magic who takes the time to read a Grimoire or other magical work from the sixteenth or seventeenth century will quickly realize that much of what is professed is no longer relevant and that much of the power that once resided in the old rituals and conjurations has long since dissipated. Ritual magic, to a greater or lesser degree, has always been in flux, with the magicians of each age struggling to discover how to bring past teachings into line with the realities of their day. This is true even now. For example, much of the preparation and practice involved in ancient magical rites falls within the present-day domain of psychology. This is why there is such an emphasis on sound psychological preparation in *Foundations of Magic*.

Of course a wholesale rejection of the past makes no more sense than indiscriminately embracing it. Much of what is universal in the old teachings will always be at the foundation of true magic. As with all disciplines, it is a combination of the traditional and the contemporary that results in the most workable, effectual magic. This is the magic that is made available here.

White and Black Magic

Most people are generally familiar with these two distinctions. In the simplest terms, white magic is worked to achieve good ends through benign magical practices, and black magic involves sinister or questionable practices, often achieving sinister or questionable goals. In practice, however, these distinctions are not always so easily discerned. For instance, if you are working a spell for someone else's benefit, you may be inadequately informed about them or their situation and the very goal you are working toward may prove detrimental to them. Undesired results can also happen when working spells for yourself. Even motivated with the best of intentions, a poorly designed spell or inaccurately formulated goal can result in undesired outcomes. *Foundations of Magic* is decidedly a book of white magic. This is why considerable time is spent in cautionary procedures for forming *intentions* and working spells for other people. It is also why you will be repeatedly warned not to vary these spells unless, or until, you are experienced and skillful at spellcraft.

High and Low Magic

These terms are often used in association with magical practices and, as with the difference between white and black magic, it is difficult to be precise when discussing the distinction between the two. Generally, low magic is that which is concerned with the practical or mundane such as finding a lost object or increasing your cash flow. High magic has more to do with personal and spiritual growth and includes things such as learning to live in alignment with your *higher self* and increasing your personal power. Many of the spells in this book don't necessarily fall neatly into either category; for example, the spell Attracting the Right Love Partner (page 96).

Magic and Power

Individuals who use magic skillfully can become quite powerful. This rightfully troubles some people who may be concerned about the potential for abuse. There are, however, two types of personal power: power over things and people, and the power that emanates through a person and allows them to realize their full potential in life. These are sometimes referred to as power *over* and power *through*. Some schools of magic rely heavily on power *over*, and these are more often than not the practices that give magic a bad name. The magic in *Foundations of Magic* operates on power *through*. Even if you are working a spell to change the weather, it is only effective insofar as it is in alignment with your *true nature* and the laws of nature. This is the power of self mastery, not the power of domination. Hitler and Napoleon relied upon power over, Gandhi and Jesus power through.

Magic and Science

One of the differences between this book's definition of magic and Aleister Crowley's definition is that the word "Science" has been replaced with the word "Craft." It could be argued that magic is a science in the sense of the older, more general definition of science that is basically systematic and formulated knowledge. Given the common modern associations with the word "Science," however, it becomes misleading to describe magic using this term. In many ways magical thinking and a magical view of the world are the antithesis of scientific thinking and a scientific view of the world. Nevertheless, don't let this dichotomy between the two worldviews fool you into thinking you must choose one. Each way of thinking approaches the truth from a different perspective and both perspectives, as enlightening as they may be in their respective domains, are incomplete. Throughout history, to the present day, many great minds have embraced both ways of knowing.

Magic and Religion

There is a belief held by some that magic and magical practices stand in opposition to religion. This is a mistaken notion. All magic has its roots in traditional religious beliefs and practices: Jewish, Christian, Egyptian, Pagan, and more. For example, many of the rituals practiced by members of the Hermetic Order of the Golden Dawn[4] include biblical passages with constant reference to the power of God. Much of the magic of the Qabala comes from the study and interpretation of traditional Jewish texts and often utilizes the power associated with the various names of God. The elaborate and esoteric Enochian magic of the Elizabethan magician John Dee was based largely on prayer and communication with angels. There is essentially no branch of magic, ancient or modern, which does not stem from religious ideology and practice.

---

4. The Hermetic Order of the Golden Dawn was a Victorian society that was influential in shaping many of the ideas and practices of modern magic.

It may then seem like a contradiction that the spells in this book were designed to be nonsectarian and they do not require adherence to any religious beliefs. This has been done in an attempt to make them widely available to people of all faiths, and to be sensitive to the enormous variety of religious and spiritual practices, and to their requirements and prohibitions. There are, of course, religious doctrines that condemn any spiritual, mystical, or magical practice other than their own. For those who profess allegiance or faith to such rigid fundamentalist beliefs, whatever they may be, the magic found here is probably not for them. For the rest of us, the magic presented here is no threat. At its simplest, this magic provides practical ways to effect positive changes. At its highest, it can be an adjunct to our religious views and a means to further our spiritual path.

Believing in Magic

It is a widely accepted notion among many people, including some students of magic, that you have to believe in magic in order for it to work. This is a complete fallacy. You do not have to believe in magic in order to effectively work magic, but you must *act* as if you believe in it. This is a very important concept in the successful working of spells and one worth expanding upon. Imagine, for the sake of illustration, that you were a kind of Rip van Winkle character who fell asleep at the beginning of the nineteenth century and awoke at the end of the twentieth. Upon waking, you would inevitably be introduced to many new things. One would certainly be the automobile. You would be told that by the correct sequence of pushing on foot pedals and moving levers and a steering wheel, you could cause a machine weighing several thousand pounds to transport you around in a controlled manner at speeds far greater than any horse-drawn vehicle. You could have four responses to this:

1. You could believe this to be true and, accordingly, act as if it were true and proceed to learn the operation of the various controls. This would eventually result in you learning to drive a car.

2. You could believe this to be true, but decide not to try to operate any of the car's controls. In this case you would not learn to drive.

3. You may believe that the whole story was far-fetched and that the driving procedures described could never produce any results. This belief could easily con-

vince you to forego trying any of the operating procedures and, once again, you would not learn to drive.

4. You do not believe the story of the automobile, but you decide to play along. Despite your disbelief you operate the pedals, levers, and steering wheel exactly as instructed. In this case you would learn to drive regardless of any belief (although, by the time you were driving, your belief would probably change).

Notice that, in order to learn to drive, it is irrelevant whether you believe in the automobile or not. What is important are the following two factors: that you *act* as if automobiles are real, and it is possible to learn to how to drive them, and that you follow the correct instructions.

The same four possibilities exist when it comes to working magic. You can believe in magic and either use it or not use it; or you *cannot* believe in magic and either act as if you did and use it or simply not use it. You will become effective at working spells when you act as if magic works regardless of your beliefs. As with learning to drive a car, you must also learn the correct skills and procedures.

Many people find that they already believe in magic and find magical concepts intuitively make sense. For those of you who may still have difficulties reconciling your beliefs to the workings of magic, you are invited to *pretend* that **everything that is written in this book is true.** You will find this useful in learning how to use *Foundations of Magic.* (This is a sneak preview of the application of the *Law of Pretending,* discussed in chapter 2.) This is very similar to what you do every time you read a novel or watch a movie in which you become engrossed. You suspend your disbelief. You know the characters and events are fictional, but you suspend your disbelief and, for the time you are engaged in the story, you *pretend* it is all true. For some, a willing suspension of disbelief will make the process of learning how to cast powerful spells considerably easier.

Ritual and Ceremony

People often raise questions regarding the necessity for ritual or ceremony in magic. Let us consider some of these.

Q: What purpose does ritual serve?

A: Magic as practiced in *Foundations of Magic* achieves much of its results though a concentration of *Will*. Rituals are a specific set of procedures that enable the practitioner to focus their *Will* and direct it to the purpose at hand.

Q: Could the same results occur just by using your mind, without these involved and unfamiliar procedures?

A: In theory, yes, but in practice it is very rare and usually only achieved by people who are exceptionally skilled and experienced in magic or other forms of personal and spiritual development. We live in a material world and for the most part we must operate through the medium of that world. The elements of ritual, the movements, the words, and the objects are the material medium of magic.

Q: Why do magical ceremonies seem so foreign to my everyday life?

A: This to be expected if you are new to magic. Think of the first time you encountered any new activity such as skiing or scuba diving or the first day at a new school or job. Everything felt unfamiliar and possibly uncomfortable or even embarrassing. There is a more basic reason rituals seem so different from everyday activities, however. They are designed to be so in order to make a clear demarcation between magical (or sacred) time and space, and mundane (profane) time and space. This is discussed further in the section on magic circles in chapter 3.

Q: Why a particular ritual for a particular spell and not any number of other possible rituals?

A: A variety of different rituals can be used to more or less achieve this same result, but effective rituals most often have a basis in tradition. In part, the traditions have developed through time as a result of magicians keeping track of what was effective and what was not. There are also guiding principles for designing new spells or modifying existing magical rituals and spells. These principles have been derived from various sources, including historical documents, oral traditions, the practiced observations of contemporary students of magic and reportedly, on rare occasions, from direct communication by adepts with spirits or other divine sources. The rituals in *Foundations of Magic* have all been carefully designed for maximum effectiveness in their respective goals.

Words of Power

The practice of using special words that are thought to have magical power is very old. In recorded history, the idea dates back at least to the magical traditions of ancient Egypt and the legend of Isis and Osiris. The legend tells of Isis resurrecting her dead husband Osiris using the magical words given her by the god Thoth. Qabalistic traditions of mysticism and magic often make use of the great power considered inherent in the various names of God, finding special power in the four-letter Hebrew name for God, יהוה, referred to as the "Tetragrammaton." The basic idea is that there are words, which for a variety of reasons, are inherently imbued with power. If the words are spoken, this power can be tapped and directed toward achieving desired results. In many older traditions these words were kept a guarded secret among a privileged few.

Neither secrecy nor a belief in the inherent power of any specific words, however, is required to exploit the magical power of words. In *Foundations of Magic,* with few exceptions, it is in the relationship of words, one to the other, and in the resonance of their sounds and in the manner in which they are spoken where their inherent power rests. This has always been true wherever the spoken word has been used effectively and it is especially true in magic. The words used in casting spells are the primary means of tapping into the unconscious and focusing and concentrating the *Will* to achieve a specific purpose. In *Foundations of Magic,* the words have been chosen very carefully to work in a variety of ways beyond the obvious literal meaning they convey. The rhythm and euphonious quality of many of the incantations, or the use of uncommon or archaic words, evoke certain moods or states that are in harmony with the purpose of the spell. Many of the spoken portions of the spells incorporate rhyme, which operates at several levels. Rhyme assists in memorizing spoken incantations, provides sound and sight metaphors for universal patterns, and acts as an attraction for the meaningful coincidences at work in magic. Rhyme, in fact, elicits and builds its own inherent kind of magical power.

The crafting of the words in a spell so as to accumulate and focus maximum power *Will* to the objective at hand is a good example of where the "Art and Craft" of magic can be appreciated. The very purposeful way in which words in this book have been chosen and placed offers another good reason not to vary these spells.

The Astral Plane and Astral Travel

Many Western esoteric traditions teach that most magical transformations manifest first in the astral plane. Varying and sometimes conflicting descriptions and explanations of the astral plane abound. Essentially it is a realm or dimension of nonphysicality, yet events that occur there are reported to have a profound effect on a person's life. It is a place where your physical body can never go but your astral body can. Your astral body is said to be part of your normal makeup and allows you to separate your consciousness from your physical body, thus freeing it to travel in dimensions of time and space free of normal physical limitations. This is referred to as "astral traveling" or "astral projection."

Many people who practice magic experience the astral plane as every bit as real as the everyday physical plane. Others question its reality and claim that it does not exist separate from our imaginations. Still others maintain that it is semireality, transcendent reality, or parallel reality. It is not important for our purposes, however, to enter into any deliberations about the reality of the astral plane or the astral body. What is of interest here is to make use of some of the special characteristics of astral travel. Of particular interest is the notion that several aspects of yourself can be in separate locations at the same time. To get an idea of this, imagine that you do have an astral body that is usually joined with your physical body, but which can separate at will. Take a moment and visualize that your astral body, complete with your consciousness, drifts up and out of your physical body and hovers somewhere near the ceiling (or if you happen to be outside when you read this, hovers several feet above your physical body). In your imagination look up and see your astral body hovering over you. Now switch perspectives and visualize that you are looking down *from* your astral body and you can see your physical body sitting or standing below you. There are now two of you.

Variations of this mental exercise of the two "yous" (the simultaneous awareness of the astral "you" that can travel about free of physical constraints and the "you" in your physical body) come into play in several of the spells in *Foundations of Magic*.

Your True Nature or Higher Self

To repeat what has already been stated, your *true nature*, sometimes called your *higher self*, refers to your nature free of the distortions or internal conflicts caused by beliefs, personality, culture, and the other psychological and psychic adornments that we all take on in order to get by in the world. Realizing your *higher self* and the resultant freedom from internal conflicts, even if it is just for the period of time it takes to prepare for and cast your spell, is a prerequisite for working effective magic. In the chapters that follow you will learn about the preparations required before casting a spell, the procedures for ascending to a *higher state* and the method of creating magical space by casting a magic circle. All of these activities are designed to ensure that you are in touch with the essential aspects of your *higher self* and *true nature*. It is from such a state that you will work your most effective magic. Fully realizing your *true nature* can be thought of as the long-term goal of all forms of personal and spiritual growth work, and it is the goal of any committed practitioner of magic. It is a transcendent goal analogous to the desire for enlightenment in Buddhism, becoming one with God in the Judaeo-Christian traditions, or any of the paths toward transcendent unity that exist in most religious and mystical traditions.

This does not mean that you must intentionally be on a path toward transcendence or spiritual growth in order to effectively work these spells. This is a book of practical magic and it is intended to be used to address everyday concerns. Working these spells, however, will open a door to this path if you so choose. Whenever you use the powerful, gentle magic of *Foundations of Magic* to effect changes in your life, you will develop and grow a little, and you will discover new things about yourself and your world. If you practice magic long enough, you will begin to notice a curious and seemingly paradoxical phenomenon; the more you realize and live in harmony with your *true nature*, the less you will need to work magic rituals to improve your life.

Theory vs. Practice

There are examples of magical traditions where philosophy and theory play an important role. In some forms of Qabalism, intellectual pursuits and contemplations are at the core of the system. Much magic, however, is based on practical need, and many of the more powerful magical rites have been derived through the use of strictly empirical methods. In other words, if it works it must be true, and so use it again. What this meant in practice was that often the magician as well as the person for whom a spell was being cast did not know why the magic worked. Many powerful magicians were not philosophers. This is similar to the issue of believing or not believing in magic. You do not need to know why a magical spell works in order for it to be effective. Once again, the analogy of the automobile is appropriate. Most people do not fully understand the internal workings of an automobile and some have no understanding at all, yet they can drive competently. If there are explanations in this book that you don't understand or find lacking, this will not affect your ability to work magic.

Some Problems with Success

Frequently, even those who believe in magic are astonished by the effectiveness of the spells in *Foundations of Magic*. Success in working magic and achieving your goals often comes quickly. With success, however, can come problems. In particular, be alert to the following potential pitfalls:

1. You can start to believe that you are a magician. You are not. Becoming a magician requires dedication, study and aptitude. These spells have been carefully designed so that anyone who adequately prepares and follows the prescribed procedures will succeed. It is as if you read the instructions for installing a new software program into your computer, followed the instructions, and succeeded in having the software work, and then considered yourself a computer programmer. This is not to say that you cannot become either a computer programmer or a magician if you so chose, but you must embark on the course of study necessary for proficiency in either pursuit.

2. You are so pleased with the results that you feel the need to talk to other people about everything you are doing. Don't. One of the basic edicts in magic is "Keep Silent." Magic works best when left alone and not discussed. There are two exceptions to the "Keep Silent" rule. First, if there is someone whom you believe could benefit from working with spells then making a suggestion to that effect is all right if you find an appropriate moment to present such a suggestion, and if you refrain from trying to sell the idea. Second, if you know other people who are engaged in magical practices, it is generally appropriate to discuss your activities with them for the purposes of learning more and improving your skills. Remember that you must never divulge any information given to you in confidence.

3. Despite your commitment to silence, word may get around that you have made some remarkable changes in your life, or perhaps you have successfully helped someone else and you gain a measure of notoriety. This can become a problem

for you if you let it go to your head. Ironically, an inflated ego stemming from success at working magic will result in you becoming less successful at working magic. If you find that you genuinely enjoy helping other people then it is time to consider pursuing a serious course of study in magic and psychology. Your knowledge and experience need to be much greater than you can acquire by achieving success with *Foundations of Magic.*

Magical Symbols, Substances, and Implements

Symbols and substances with magical properties or consecrated magical implements are another means by which to concentrate power and focus *Will* to a purpose. These are used, although sparingly, in *Foundations of Magic.* As with the spoken words in these spells, the symbols, substances, and implements have been carefully chosen. Magical symbols and other accessories can take many forms and many explanations can be offered as to why they are considered useful or necessary. Sometimes the connection between the symbols or objects and the purpose of a spell are obvious, as when a photograph of someone is used. Sometimes the connections are less than obvious, as with the magical properties of some herbs or signs. Consistency regarding this subject is often lacking, and within the same or similar magical traditions one can find disagreement on the proper meaning or use of various symbols and substances. An understanding of why certain symbols or other embellishments are part of any particular ritual in this book is not necessary for their effectiveness. For the most part, explanations of such are cursory or absent.

Some Laws of Magic

There are a number of magical laws upon which *Foundations of Magic* is based. Six of these laws are described below. Knowledge of the first five is not essential to successfully working the spells, but they will prove useful in furthering your understanding of the magic you are about to work. Understanding and adhering to the sixth law, the *Law of Prudence,* is essential. In a magical worldview, these are laws of nature. In a scientific worldview, they are decidedly not.

The Law of Will

Will is intention that is in complete harmony with an individual's *true nature* or *higher self*. *Will* is a powerful force and can influence events in the world in two ways:

It can act directly as an agent of change.

It can initiate and direct other agents of change.

The more concentrated and focused the *Will* is to a purpose, the greater its power to achieve that purpose.

The Law of Levels

This is perhaps best stated in the famous pronouncement on the Emerald Tablet attributed to the legendary magician of ancient times, Hermes Trismegistus: "What is below is like that which is above, and what is above is like that which is below." This law is at the foundation of designing effective spells, for the rituals, words and objects in a spell are but a microcosm of some aspect of the universe, and when a purpose is realized within the time and space of working a spell, it is realized in the universe as a whole. Another implication of this law is the notion that every individual is a microcosm of the entire universe and every aspect of a person has a corresponding aspect in the universe as a whole. This is the basis for the goal of attaining full recognition and realization of your *true nature*, for then you become one with the universe of which you are a complete microcosm.

The First Law of Association

Sometimes simply stated as "like attracts like," this is the law of sympathetic magic. Things that have properties in common with each other can attract or influence each other. For example, the spell to attract rain (Bringing the Rain, page 216) uses the similarity between rainwater and sparkling wine to assist in achieving the purpose.

The Second Law of Association

Objects or substances that have had contact with each other will continue to affect each other after they are separated. The more intimate the original contact, the greater the effect after separation. This, for instance, is why a person's hair or an animal's fur is so often used in spells. This is the magic that is at work in the spell Helping Your Distressed Plant or Animal (page 211).

The Law of Correspondences

Throughout the history of magic, students and practitioners have attempted to determine magical correspondences between two or more symbols or entities. For example, the herb basil corresponds with the planet Mars, which in turn corresponds to the color red, which corresponds to the direction South. What this means is that each of these things—basil, Mars, red, and South—embody some similar magical attributes or universal characteristics. In some ways this is like *The First Law of Association*, except that the similarities are not so directly apparent to our senses. It is not readily apparent upon physical examination what basil may have in common with Mars. Correspondences are used to concentrate influences relevant to the purpose of a spell, for example, to help achieve its aim. The spell Attracting the Right Love Partner (page 96) uses the correspondence of the color yellow to the Sun, which in turn has a correspondence to truth.

The Law of Prudence

Magic is most effective if practiced in concert with all other prudent measures. In other words, unless there is apparently no alternative, don't rely exclusively on magical spells to achieve your goals. For example, if you suffer from depression, seek professional help in addition to working the spell Eliminating Depression or the Blues (page 179).

Corollary to the Law of Prudence. Neglecting to take prudent steps to achieve a goal belies the *intention* to achieve that goal. Magic is futile when directed to realize an *intention* your actions do not support.

2

THE PSYCHOLOGY OF MAGIC

Psychology, as the term is being used in this book, refers to the knowledge and understanding of mental and emotional process and behavior. Although the connection between psychology and magic may not always be obvious, the two are and always have been inseparable. In fact, in past eras there was often no distinction made between them. Much of what we would consider as belonging firmly in the realm of psychological knowledge and practice was previously thought an inseparable part of the magical arts. To change a person's behavior or emotional state was work for a magician, as was the preparation to ready a person's psyche to engage in magical practices or receive the benefits of magical works. Today, of course, psychology stands as an established set of disciplines on its own. Many, if not most, psychologists would resist any but the most tentative and metaphorical associations with magic. Nevertheless the truth remains, that anyone who desires proficiency in the magical arts must be skilled in the necessary psychological knowledge, skills, and practices.

The often-used metaphor of a seed can be useful in explaining the role of psychology in working magic. Indeed, a seed is magical both figuratively and literally. The apple seed, for instance, is less than a quarter of an inch in its largest dimension, and yet it has the power to transform air, water, and earth into an ever-changing, living sculpture of wood and vegetation a million times the seed's own mass. If the soil is depleted or poorly conditioned, the seed will fail to thrive, and if the soil is too impoverished the seed may sprout, but will shortly wither and die. The analogy applies to magical works. The soil in which the seed of magic is planted corresponds to the psychological state of the person working the magic. Even the strongest magic will fail to take hold if the person who is working it is psychologically ill prepared to receive and nurture the transformations it delivers.

There are countless volumes, both in and out of publication, that provide the words and describe the procedures for working innumerable spells. Beyond providing entertainment or academic interest however, the usefulness of such publications is limited to those who are already experienced and skillful in the magical arts. Without the proper mental and emotional training and preparation, one cannot expect to simply follow the recipe out of a book and perform powerfully effective magic. It is the careful attention to this preparation that sets this work apart from most other works on spellcraft. As mentioned previously, using *Foundations of Magic* will not turn you into a magician. For this you will need dedicated study and practice. What it does offer is a quick and efficient way to gain the skills and make the necessary preparations required to work the specific spells within their covers. This is unique.

The specific psychological preparations required to work effective magic are different for each spell, and are individually addressed in the instructions for each spell in Part II. This chapter provides a discussion of the concepts that are necessary to understand these instructions. It also includes simple exercises that will provide you with firsthand experience in applying the concepts. Conscientiously completing each exercise is an essential part of learning the skills necessary to successfully work the magic in *Foundations of Magic*.

The subject of the psychology of magic is vast. This chapter merely touches on the subject and, limits its scope to just what is necessary or useful for using this book.

The Law of Pretending

This is an important concept in learning magic or any other skill. You will see it referred to often in this book. The most concise statement of the *Law of Pretending* has been attributed to the late Milton Erickson, a remarkable hypnotherapist who was often referred to by his admirers as a magician. Erickson said:

"If you *pretend* anything well enough, you can master it."

To understand this statement, the meaning of the word "*pretend*" must be made clear. Many people associate pretending with acting one way while feeling another. For instance, you may smile and compliment someone on their new Carmen Miranda hat[1] all the while finding it hideous, or you may go into a job interview and outwardly behave and talk as if you are sure of yourself while actually feeling a complete lack of confidence. This is only half pretending. Complete pretending requires that you *pretend* on the inside as well as on the outside.

To understand how to go about this, take the example of the Carmen Miranda hat. To begin, adopt the attitude that it would be interesting to have the experience of liking a hat that looks like a fruit bowl. After all, the person wearing it likes it, so it must be possible. Next, think of a hat that you really do like. When you get in touch with the experience of really liking a hat, hold onto that feeling and continue to hold onto it while you see or imagine the Miranda hat. Now your pretending can be complete. You can look at the Carmen Miranda hat, smile, hold onto the feeling of liking a hat and say you like the hat. At this point your experience is essentially the same as if you did like the hat.

Similarly, in the example of the job interview, you can first think of some arena in your life where you are confident. This can be absolutely any situation where you are confident. If asked to pick up a baseball off the ground, anyone not physically hindered in some way would be confident that they can do this. Of course going to a job interview and picking up a baseball are two entirely different things, but the experience of being confident is always just the experience of being confident. It doesn't matter what the situation is. Once you have the experience in one situation, you need only hold on to the feeling in another situation such as going to a job interview. It is often difficult for people to fully grasp the implications of this. If you can feel confident in any one situation, then you can *pretend* to feel confident in any other situation, and when you *pretend* well enough you will be confident in that situation. Sometimes this may take a little practice or rehearsal. This process is exactly what actors do when getting into character. You will be surprised at just how quickly you can catch on.

Pretending can also be useful in learning new skills. For example, in the exercises that follow and later in the instructions for working specific spells, you will sometimes be asked to form a mental picture of someone or something. Some people are

---

1. Carmen Miranda was a Latin singer and dancer who appeared in movies in the 1940s. Her costume almost always included a hat that was covered with artificial fruit.

not consciously aware of their mental images, and therefore don't think they can form a picture in their mind. All they need do in this case is *pretend* that they see their mental pictures. This often allows the person to become consciously aware of mental images and, if not, it still results in the desired outcome of the exercise even if there is no conscious awareness of how that occurred.

People are often concerned with the idea of pretending because they believe that they would not be truthful either with themselves or with others. This concern arises from confusion between pretending and acting fraudulently. Fraud is the portraying of yourself or the facts in some way that is inaccurate in order to achieve some goal. If you flatter someone in order to win their favor, for instance by telling them you like their hat when you really don't, that is fraud. This is different than getting in touch with a useful or positive experience, such as liking a hat, and applying it to other situations for the purposes of learning or improving the way you feel about things. This is pretending. Elaborating on the example of the job interview may help clarify this distinction.

> **Fraud:** You falsify your resume to show you have more experience than you do. Outwardly you act confident during the interview when in fact you are experiencing a distinct lack of confidence.

> **Pretending:** You present accurate information on your resume in a manner that puts you in the best light based on the truth. During the interview you *pretend* you are confident by holding onto the experience of being confident, which you normally have in some other area of your life.

Referring back to the discussion of power in chapter 1, fraud is an example of attempting to gain power *over* and pretending is an example of power *through*. If you are still unsure about the difference, remember that pretending does not require that you lie about anything.

One of the most important characteristics of pretending well is to be 100 percent committed to the role for the time you are in character. In order to get the full benefit from pretending, you must hold nothing back. No part of you must be reserved or unsure that this is a good role. People are often afraid to commit to anything 100 percent because they are not sure it is right. This is the wonderful thing about pretending. If you find you don't care for the experience, you can simply stop pretending, or you can *pretend* something else. If you do find that your new role fits you well, or improves your life, you can just keep on pretending until the line between pretending and your normal experience naturally fades and vanishes. One of the lovely common occurrences when pretending is incorporated with magic is that people often find that what they are pretending is more in line with their *true nature* than what they have been used to doing. This is the basic reason the Law of Pretending is referred to so often in this book.

The Unconscious Mind

One of the most frequently used terms in this chapter is "unconscious mind." There are many different descriptions in the realm of psychology as to exactly what this means and many different explanations about how the unconscious functions. Sometimes psychologists make very fine distinctions between similar terms such as "not conscious," "subconscious," and "preconscious," and expound on how they all relate to unconsciousness and consciousness. For our purposes, the operational definition of unconscious mind and an explanation of its role are simple:

Any activity of your mind or brain of which you are not consciously aware or which you cannot consciously control is the work of your unconscious mind.

The following are some examples of the two types of unconscious processing. Some of these unconsciously generated experiences may not apply to you, but similar ones will.

Consciously Unaware:
- The last ten times you shifted in your chair or blinked your eyelids.

- How you find the answer in your memory to the question, "What is the largest and most famous city in France?"

- Much of what you do when you drive a car (unless you are just learning to drive).

- Almost all of what you do when you walk.

- The knowledge required to construct a spoken sentence in English.

- The knowledge required to do almost any routine task.

- Much of the mental activity and information processing required to solve a difficult problem or to realize an intention.

- The internal mental and emotional workings that result in well-established patterns of behavior.

- Most of what is going on in your own brain.

Out of Conscious Control:
- The urge to have a chocolate bar or smoke a cigarette.

- Your dislike of the color chartreuse.

- That damn tune that keeps running through your head.

- Being sexually attracted to someone.

- Fear of spiders.

- Love.

All of us have our behavior and our ongoing experience governed to a great extent by our unconscious mind. So what is the function of our unconscious mind?

The unconscious mind is in charge of automating tasks that are routine or tasks of such complexity that they would overwhelm the conscious mind. It is also in charge of ensuring that our basic human needs are met at their most fundamental level.

To state the obvious, your unconscious mind is in charge of many aspects of your life and cannot be ignored if you are intending to make significant changes. Both effective psychology and effective magic embrace the unconscious mind as a necessary and welcome ally in change. This will become apparent as you become more familiar with *Foundations of Magic.*

The Conscious Mind

What then is the conscious mind? Oddly, this is a difficult question to answer with any satisfaction. The most immediate answer is that the conscious mind is the vehicle by which we are aware of our experiences. This, however, is somewhat circular and not a particularly useful reply. A more philosophical answer, and one that is more suited to the purposes of working magic, is:

Our conscious mind is the seat of our free *Will* and the place where we form our *intentions*.

Conscious-Unconscious Mind Agreement

The question then arises, "What happens when our conscious and unconscious minds disagree?" The answer to this is quite straightforward. Unless the disagreement is resolved, our conscious mind can have things its way for a short time, but our unconscious mind will always win out in the end. This brings us to one of the most important principles of psychology: **The most effective way to accomplish anything is to have your conscious and unconscious minds in complete agreement.** Securing this agreement is the primary goal of the psychological preparations that precede each spell and is also a consideration in the design of the rituals in magic.

Although it may be apparent by now, one last characteristic of our unconscious mind needs to be mentioned here. It does not do things in the same way as our conscious mind. Symbols, metaphors, paradox, intuition, rhyme and rhythm, nonsense, connections of great complexity, multileveled meanings and myth are but a few of the tools and communication channels favored by the unconscious mind. Rational thought, logic, well-constructed sentences, literal meanings, consistency and the illusions of order and control are more to the liking of the conscious mind. It is no mystery, then, on which side magic weighs in.

Problems, Unconscious Parts, and Benefits

There are two different kinds of experiences that we commonly think of as problems: Those that occur randomly, often outside of your control, and those that re-occur or form a pattern in our lives. The former are more accurately called "difficulties" and the latter "problems." Examples of difficulties are a skiing accident (unless of course you are accident prone and this sort of thing happens regularly), a downturn in the economy, a loss (such as a death in the family), an overbearing employer, or your car breaking down. Examples of problems are extreme shyness, an addiction to cigarettes, constantly fighting with your spouse, and chronic guilt.

Despite the obvious negative consequences, almost all difficulties and problems bring some benefits, or at least the promise of benefits. The benefits derived from difficulties are generally more accidental and incidental. A broken leg may provide a much needed rest from work or the loss of a loved one may come with new learning and a shift in your priorities.

On the other hand, the benefits, or perceived benefits, from problems are purposeful, at least at the unconscious level. Being shy can be a form of protection—a way to prevent you from doing or saying something that embarrasses you or which offends someone. Smoking can reduce tension in social or work environments, curb your appetite and temporarily offer relief from negative feelings. Fighting with your spouse can be seen to preserve your own sense of identity, protect your interests and, paradoxically, can be an attempt to rid yourself of the bad feelings that originally caused the fight. The list is endless and varies from one individual to another and from one type of problem to another.

When people are first introduced to this concept it is often difficult for them to comprehend why anyone would choose such a method of achieving a benefit, particularly if they are dealing with a problem that brings serious consequences. For example, smoking may help you to relax, but it also ruins your health, is expensive, and leaves your clothes, hair, and breath all smelling like an ashtray. Surely there must be a better way.

To begin to make sense of this, it is useful to consider much of a person's behavior as being under the control of various unconscious parts of that person. For example, people have an unconscious part that is in charge of getting enough rest, relieving tension, getting work completed, eating the right food, protecting themselves from emotional and physical pain, and countless other very human needs and desires. These unconscious parts are sometimes more and sometimes less successful at accomplishing their goal, but they are always present and their intention is only to serve the individual. Often a part is in charge of its own department without regard for how it affects any other part.

What goes on in some large hospitals provides an analogy. We have all heard stories of someone who is sick or injured going into an emergency ward and, regardless of the pain or anguish involved, is first required by the receptionist to answer questions not related to their medical condition, fill out forms, prove their identity, establish they have insurance and wait for their family doctor to be contacted before their medical condition is even considered. The administration policymakers who dictate the procedures the receptionist must follow are primarily concerned with ensuring that the hospital gets paid, not that a person's affliction is tended to. This is similar to an unconscious part in charge of meeting a certain need. For example, for someone who wishes to quit smoking, there may be a part whose job is to relieve tension (or any number of other benefits smokers derive). This part uses a compulsion to smoke as a reliable way to relieve tension but it has no connection or concern with issues of preventing illness, saving money, or personal hygiene.

Each of our unconscious parts that is charged with taking care of one or more of our various needs is loyally and dutifully tenacious and is not willing to let go of a behavior unless it is completely satisfied that some other behavior will serve that need at least as well. These parts are extremely conservative, not trusting to newfangled ideas. Without compelling evidence to the contrary, they stick with the way they first learned to do things as the only way. Remember these parts are not the enemy. They are parts of ourselves which, misguided though they may sometimes be in their means, are intending to serve us by ensuring basic needs are met. So often people attempt to solve a problem by simply eliminating some unwanted behavior. For instance, a person will stop smoking in order to eliminate the problems associated with it. Unless another unconsciously satisfying method is found for meeting the need which precipitated the behavior, in due time the part in charge of fulfilling this need will inevitably see to it that person will again smoke. Any approach to solving a personal problem, which does not in some manner take these unconscious forces into account, is doomed to failure.

In the hospital analogy it is like trying to solve the problem of delivering prompt medical care by firing the receptionist. The administrator in charge of hospital finances will just hire another one to carry out his or her policies, and rightly so. After all, the hospital could provide no medical care if it did not have the financial means to operate. For a lasting resolution, a policy would have to be developed that would ensure *both* prompt medical attention *and* sound fiscal management. Similarly, resolving personal problems requires that we respect and even appreciate the intention of the part that is in charge and that we adopt a means of changing which satisfies this part and takes into account all of our needs. This is true in psychology as well as in magic. All too often in both disciplines, a coarse effort is made to simply eliminate or erase unpleasantries with no consideration of any inherent value that may be present.

There is one more issue that must be considered when discussing the benefits and services deriving from problems. Occasionally the problem no longer offers any real benefits. Either the need for the benefit no longer exists, or the problem behavior stops providing the benefit. The former situation exists when your life circumstances change in a way that eliminates the need. This is common with behavior that is learned in early in childhood. For example, as a small child you may have been terrified by irrational fears at night. Your young unconscious mind may have decided that the best way to protect you was to keep you vigilant at night by ensuring that you did not sleep well or long. As an adult your habit persists even though the fears and the perceived threat from which you were protecting yourself have long since passed. Now, instead of vigilance, this unconsciously controlled habit is experienced as insomnia and sleep depravation. An alcoholic in the latter stages of that affliction provides a good example of someone for whom the problem no longer provides any benefit. For example, drinking moderately can provide a sense of wellbeing in stressful situations. When social drinking deteriorates over time into chronic alcoholism, the sense of wellbeing derived from drinking is lost and is replaced by a sense of desperation to not feel sick from withdrawal. Whether the need is gone or the benefit is gone, what is common in both situations is the fact that the unconscious part in charge perceives that a need or a benefit still exists and persists with the problem behavior in an attempt to serve the individual.

Problems, their consequences and benefits, and the unconscious parts of us responsible for them, is a large subject and clearly beyond the scope of this brief introduction. Four factors are relevant here for working good magic:

1. Problems come with benefits, actual or intended.

2. An unconscious part of us is in charge of each problem.

3. The intention of all of our unconscious parts is to serve real or perceived needs.

4. Problems are not adequately resolved without satisfying the unconscious part in charge.

EXERCISE I   APPRECIATING YOUR PROBLEMS

The purpose of this exercise is to provide you with some direct experience of appreciating some of the good intentions behind your own problems. Find a quiet place where you will not be disturbed and where you can reflect and write. On a piece of paper make three columns. In the first column write down one of your own personal problems. In the second column write down the negative consequences of the problem.

Now imagine the unconscious part of you that is charge of this problem. See if you can get in touch with this part in some intuitive way. If you have difficulty doing this, just *pretend* that you are in communication with the part. As odd as it may seem, genuinely thank that part for its intention to serve you so faithfully with benefits. Ask that part if it will reveal what those intended benefits are. In the third column write down the benefits this part is intending to provide. If you don't think you know, make up some answers. Do this for several personal problems. Remember the difference between difficulties and problems, and just list the problems.

Thoughts and Feelings

Our thoughts and feelings are usually taken for granted, and for good reason; they comprise a big part of our ongoing experience. To become skilled at working magic, however, often requires conscious awareness, management, and mastery of our thoughts and feelings. Fortunately, becoming familiar with a few simple concepts and practicing several simple procedures can achieve the mastery required to use this book.

Our thoughts are made up of the pictures we make in our imagination, the words (or sounds) we hear or say in our minds and, to some extent, our feelings. If you were able to completely subtract your mental images, sounds, and feelings from your mind, you would have no thoughts or emotions. You would, in fact, have no internal experience.

Feelings themselves are very direct body experiences and, although they are often evoked by what you perceive in your surroundings, they are more frequently governed by what you are thinking. For instance, you can feel joy at the birth of your first child, a one-time event. You can also re-experience a version of this joy many times by simply remembering it. The same is true with unpleasant feelings. Often people will go through the day, or even many days, feeling bad because they continue to think about some disagreeable event or situation that happened in the past, or that may happen in the future, and is completely removed from them at the moment. In these cases thoughts, rather than the direct experiences, are generating feelings. Let us take a closer look at the various components of our thoughts.

Images

Broadly speaking, there are two kinds of images people create in their mind: remembered images and constructed images. In order to be able to adequately answer the question, "what does your car look like?" you must see a *remembered* image of your car in your mind. If you are asked to imagine what your house would look like if it were colored day-glo orange, you would have to *construct* such an image in your mind, even though presumably you have never seen such a sight. All people (except those who were born blind) rely on both kinds of mental images countless times every day. The form and quality of images, however, varies dramatically from person to person, and within the same person depending on what they are thinking about.

Sounds

There are also remembered and constructed sounds in our thoughts. You can recall the sound of your mother's voice or of a trumpet playing (remembered) and in your mind you can probably hear what your mother's voice might sound like if she were a man (constructed). In addition to these two categories of sound, we also hear the sound of self-talk in our minds. In your mind (not out loud), tell yourself, "take out the garbage," or recite the nursery rhyme "Mary Had a Little Lamb." This is self-talk.

Feelings

There are a number of different types of body feelings we can re-experience in our mind: for instance, touch, movement, and position. What would it feel like to have someone touch you on the left shoulder right now? Notice that even though no one is actually touching you, in your mind you can feel what it is like. What would it feel like to slowly raise your right arm until it is pointing straight up in the air? Your mind can feel that movement, and the new mental position of your arm, even though your arm remains stationary in its original position.

In addition to these body sensations which are referred to as feelings, people also experience emotional feelings such as sadness, joy, fear, and pain (hurt feelings). Many people find it quite easy to get in touch with an entire range of emotional feelings at almost any time. Good actors are so adept at this that when they are in character they are actually experiencing the feelings that character would feel in the circumstances of the role. For other people this seems quite difficult. Exercise 4 (page 44) and Exercise 5 (page 46) provides an effective method for allowing people to gain access to a wide variety of feelings.

Modes that are Out of Consciousness

Many people will object that they do not see pictures in their mind, or that they only think in pictures and never think in words, or that they can never get in touch with their feelings. With few exceptions, as with people who are born blind or deaf, everyone thinks in all modes: pictures, words, sounds, and feelings. Quite often, however, one of these modes is out of consciousness. A bit of reflection will reveal that this has to be the case. Take for example people who say they don't see pictures in their mind. If such people are asked to described the front of the house or building in which they live, they can. Where did they get that information—that *visual* information? It comes from looking at some sort of mental image of the front of their home, whether that image is in their consciousness or not.

EXERCISE 2   BECOMING FAMILIAR WITH MODES
                                       OF THINKING AND FEELING

These exercises are designed to increase your awareness of your own thinking and feeling processes. If one of your thinking modes occurs outside of your consciousness, this exercise will often help to bring it into consciousness. At the very least you will become aware of what is and what is not consciously available to you at this time. To some people these exercises may seem easy or even trivial. If this is the case for you, then you are fortunate, for you are already quite aware of many of your own mental and emotional processes. Those who have difficulty with parts of this exercise can invoke the *Law of Pretending*. For instance, if you find it hard to bring your mental images into consciousness, or if you have a problem forming clear mental images, simply *pretend* that you can.

Remembered Images

1. What does da Vinci's painting "Mona Lisa" look like?

2. How is the checkout laid out at your local supermarket?

3. What is the first thing you see when you look in your closet?

4. What did you look like in the mirror when you were ten years old?

5. What does a tiger look like?

Constructed Images

1. What would the Eiffel Tower look like if it had been built upside down and was standing on its point?

2. What would your bedroom look like if all the walls were painted bright red?

3. How would you look in a bullfighter's outfit?

4. What would your mother look like if she were a man?

5. What would this page look like if it were made of pale orange, processed cheese?

Remembered Sounds

1. What does your mother's voice sound like?

2. What does a barking dog sound like?

3. Tap the nearest hard surface and wait thirty seconds. What did that tap sound like?

4. Listen to a favorite piece of classical or instrumental music in your mind.

Constructed Sounds

1. What would a bucketful of golf balls falling on a tin roof sound like?

2. What would the national anthem sound like played on 100 accordions?

3. What is the sound of two pies colliding in midair during a pie fight?

4. What would a busy freeway sound like if all automobiles were powered with wind-up rubber band motors?

Self Talk—Do the following in words in your mind, not out loud.

1. Recite your full name.

2. Question whether or not you are a loser. (In other words say, "I'm a loser.")

3. Tell yourself that you are a success.

4. Sing the words to "Sgt. Pepper's Lonely Hearts Club Band" (or any other song with lyrics).

5. Ask yourself, "What could this possibly mean?"

Feelings—Body Sensations

1. What would it feel like to have a fly land on the back of your hand?

2. Feel your right foot immersed in ice water.

3. Feel what it would be like to lift both hands over your head and grab onto a chinning bar, and then feel the muscle strain in both arms as you do a chin-up.

4. Feel what it would be like to fall out of a two-story window and land safely on a trampoline.

5. What does your stomach feel like when you have overeaten?

Feelings—Emotional

1. Remember a time when you were a little sad. (Do not pick a major or devastating event in your life.) Feel what that was like to be sad.

2. Do the same, except replace sadness with joy.

3. Think of a time when you were quite confident about something. Feel now what that confidence felt like.

4. Think of a time when you were nervous or had butterflies. Feel what that felt like.

Participants, Observers, and Memories

There is a qualitative difference in being a *participant* and being an *observer* in any activity. In order to appreciate this difference experientially, imagine the following scene. There is a car parked at the top edge of a sheer precipice. Over the precipice is a 1,000 foot drop to a river below. Visualize that you are looking at this scene and in your imagination watch as the driver starts the car and drives it slowly up to and over the edge of the cliff. Watch the car with the driver inside fall to the water below. Now replay this scene, but this time you are the driver and you are seeing it as it happens from inside the car. First see the view out of the windshield. Notice your hands in front of you on the steering wheel. Feel the steering wheel in your hands and feel your body weight pressing down on the car seat. Feel your right hand reach for and turn on the ignition key. Hear the sound of the motor as you start it up and drive toward the cliff. See the view through windshield as you move closer to the edge. Feel the car shift dramatically as the front wheels leave the ground and then experience the weightlessness of free fall as you accelerate toward the water.

The second experience, that of the participant, is much more experientially stimulating and emotionally charged than the first. Although there are exceptions, it is generally true that being a *participant* is more emotionally charged than being an observer. This is true even if you are observing yourself. Imagine the first part of the scene again as the *observer*, but this time imagine that somehow it is you in the driver's seat as well as you observing. (This is a version of the two "yous" mentioned in the discussion of astral travel in chapter 1, page 20.) Remember that you are still viewing this event from a safe distance, even though it is you in the car. It is as if you are seeing yourself do this on a video. Notice that it is not nearly as exciting as when you are experiencing it from the position of a *participant* inside the car.

The same phenomenon occurs in our memories. Some people normally experience their memories as an *observer* and others regularly experience them as a *participant*. In order to determine how you tend to remember things, do the following exercise.

EXERCISE 3

Remember the following three events:

1. The last time you were in a frightening situation (for instance, a close call in a car).

2. Any event that occurred when you were about ten years old.

3. The last time you brushed your teeth.

Notice the mental images associated with each memory. (If you are someone who isn't consciously aware of mental images, then just *pretend* you have a image for each memory.) As you remember these images, do you see yourself in the memory, or do you see what you saw at the time out of your own eyes? If you see an image of yourself in the memory, you are remembering things as an *observer*. Some people see only part of themselves in the memory, for example from a perspective of looking over their own shoulder from where they see the back of their own shoulder and part of the back of their own head. This is still viewing the event from the perspective of an *observer*. If you don't see yourself at all but only see an image of what you saw during the original event (through your own eyes), then you remember as a *participant*.

People who consistently remember things as an *observer* usually have a difficult time getting in touch with the feelings associated with the original event. This is neither good nor bad, but it does become an issue when they attempt to apply the *Law of Pretending*. Such a person may, for example, remember many past situations when they were confident, but be unable to reconnect with that feeling of confidence when remembering the event.

There are some people who do remember events as *participants*, but still have difficulty connecting with the feelings associated with the remembered event. This is usually the result of a memory that is incomplete in one of the modes of body sensation or sound (including talk). When you remembered the frightening situation, did you hear in memory what you heard at that time? Did you feel your body sensations (body position, touch, motion, pressure, etc.) as they were at that time? In order to fully experience the feeling component of a memory, the memory must include the three primary senses: sight (mental images), sound (what you heard including what you were saying), and body sensation.[2] This applies to more than just memory. Any time you want to experience something that isn't actually happening at the time you must see it, hear it, and touch it in your imagination. The fantasy of driving over the cliff in a car is a good example. Notice that you were instructed to touch the steering wheel and the keys, feel your weight on the seat, hear the motor, feel the movements of the car, and see what was right before your eyes.

As interesting as this discussion on memory and feelings may be, it is probably difficult at this point to know what it has to do with working magic. Applying these concepts is essential in practicing the *Law of Pretending* or in any other activity that requires a person get in touch with the feeling components of their internal experiences (thoughts, memories, fantasies, imaginings, daydreams, etc.). As will become apparent when you start working in *Foundations of Magic*, recapturing your experiences and working with them is a very important element in casting some spells. Before going on to the next exercise, it will be useful to review the two important requirements for fully experiencing your memories, including their emotional component:

1. Your memories must be **complete** in sight, sound, and body sensation.

2. The images in your memories must be from the perspective of *participant*.

EXERCISE 4   EXPERIENCING FEELINGS IN A MEMORY

In this exercise you are going to have the freedom to change some aspects of a memory very much as a film editor can determine what is seen or heard in a movie, except in this case you are *in* the movie. The goal of editing is to increase the feeling component of a memory. For those of you who find it easy to get in touch with past feelings, this exercise may not be particularly illuminating as you are probably already experiencing complete *participant* memories.

---

2. Sometimes remembering smell and, to a lesser degree taste, is essential to evoking the complete feeling component of a memory. In fact, smell is a sense that involves very little brain processing before it registers in consciousness. This means that it is more immediately and directly related to our experience. This is why some smells can evoke very strong memory feelings years after the event. For our purposes, however, remembering smell and taste are generally not necessary unless they occur spontaneously as part of a memory.

Remember a specific time when you were very nervous. It is important that this is a memory of a specific event in your life, not just a general notion that at some time in the past you were nervous. Notice the images that come with this memory. Do you see yourself in the images? Are you viewing the event from the position of *participant* or *observer*? If you see yourself (or part of yourself such as from over your own shoulder) in the memory, then in your imagination shift your viewpoint to that of the "you" in the memory. See this past event through your own eyes (as a *participant*) just as you saw it during the event. If you are someone for whom your remembered images are outside of your consciousness, then make up an image of what you were most likely seeing at the time.

Once you have made the shift from *observer* to *participant*, notice if you can hear what you heard at the time. Who was talking? What were they saying and what did their voice sound like? What were you saying? What other noises were occurring? Music? Machinery? Wind or waves? Traffic? If the sounds that were present during the event are absent from your memory, then add them. If you are not completely sure just what words were said or what sounds you heard at the time, then use your best judgment and add words and sounds you would likely have heard at the time.

Now you should have shifted the viewpoint from *observer* to *participant* and added dialog and sound effects to your memory. Are you aware of the body sensation that occurred during this event? Were you sitting or standing or lying down? Were you stationary or moving? Can you feel the weight of your feet against the floor or your body against a chair? What are your hands touching and where are they? Were you hot or cold? Once again, if you are not sure of the exact details, fill them in. Feel what your hands were likely touching. Feel the position or your body. Feel any sensation of motion that is similar to what occurred.

If you were successful in completing each step and combining sound, body sensation, and sight as a *participant*, you should be able to re-experience some of your original nervousness. Practice this again with another memory, but this time with a more pleasant experience. Remember a specific time when you were in a very good mood. As before, it is important that this is a memory of a specific event in your life. Repeat the same steps (as above) for editing this memory.

EXERCISE 5

CREATING AND EXPERIENCING
AN ARTIFICIAL MEMORY

Indulge yourself in a small fantasy. You are a retired lion trainer who has had a long and successful career. You are sitting in your home during a quiet moment, reflecting back on your experiences. You find yourself remembering the very first time you stepped into the lions' cage alone, and how nervous you were. You were an apprentice back then and the person who had been training you was sick in bed. True to tradition, the show had to go on. A large cage containing three lions was in the center ring of the circus and the house was packed. Your memory starts as you first approached the heavy metal door of the cage and were just about to open it. The goal of the exercise is for you to be able to feel the excitement and nervousness of this artificial memory.

To begin to build this memory, imagine what you would have seen at that time. See the cage and the cage door. Look through the bars of the cage and see the lions. What are the lions doing? What else is in the cage with them? Are they male or female lions? Look down and see the sawdust on the floor under your feet. Look down at what you are wearing. Look around and see the crowd and the features of the building or circus tent. Be particularly aware of the fact there are no other people close to you. You are alone. Look at your hands; do you have anything in either one of them? What is the color or colors of your shirtsleeves? Take a little while and compose a complete picture of the scene around you.

Next, consider what you would be hearing. There are obvious sounds like the roar of the lions or the cheering of the crowd. In your mind, listen to these sounds. Hear the words of the ringleader or announcer as you open the door and enter the cage. Does the cage door squeak? Do the lions make more or less noise when you enter? Do you crack a whip or talk to the lions? If you talk what do you say and how loudly do you say it? How does the crowd's response change depending on what you and the lions are doing?

Now it is time to add your body sensations. Feel the weight of your body on your feet as you stand and walk. Feel which hand is opening the gate. Is your hand holding onto a bar or a handle or a latch? Feel the resistance of the door as you open it and close it behind you. Notice the temperature of the air around you. Is it hot or cold or neither? Feel the touch and brush of your clothing on your body and limbs.

As this is *your* artificial memory, you will undoubtedly include things that are not mentioned above. Briefly rehearse the sights, sounds, and body sensations until you can put them together into one seamless memory fragment. Remember to view everything from the point of view of a *participant*. A long memory sequence is not necessary, just the few moments around approaching and opening the cage door and stepping into the cage is necessary. This is the time when you should be able to experience the excitement and nervousness that went with your solo debut.

If after completing Exercises 4 and 5 you still have difficulty experiencing the feeling component of memory, either real or artificial, let it go for now. Several days after you have read the next section (Intention, Incubation, and Letting Go), go through the steps of these exercises again. If you do this, choose different memories than those already used in Exercise 4. For example, remember a time when you felt very confident or relaxed. In Exercise 5, create a different artificial memory such as giving your acceptance speech at the Oscars or your first rocket launch from Cape Kennedy.

Intention, Incubation, and Letting Go

Intention

Will has both a magical and a psychological component; *intention* is really just the psychological component of *Will*. Even separate from magic, *intention* is a very powerful force and forming an *intention* demands careful consideration. Be sure you really want the results that realizing your *intention* will bring. The old aphorism applies here: "Be careful what you wish for; you may get it." This is never more important than when you are casting a spell. You must be very sure that when your spell works, you will like the results. Guidelines for designing a well-formed *intention* are covered in detail in the next chapter. For the purposes of this chapter it is sufficient to point out that, with or without formal magic, forming an *intention* can be very powerful, and is the first essential step in accomplishing any goal.

Incubation Time

When our *intention* is to effect a significant change in our life, it is our unconscious mind that is in charge of getting the job done. Although the mental processing remains undetected, our unconscious mind goes to work planning and preparing. It must determine which personal strengths we possess that will promote the change, and those that we lack and must develop. It examines the behaviors that need to be added to our repertoire and those that should be dropped. It evaluates those beliefs that run counter to realizing the *intention,* and those beliefs that support it. It must consider any changes we make in the light of how these changes affect other areas of our life, for better or worse.

The list of mental activities in which our unconscious mind must engage in order to realize our *intentions* is considerable, and it needs time to satisfactorily work everything out. It is our unconscious mind that is in charge, and unconscious means just that: what is going on is outside of our consciousness. It may not seem to our conscious mind that anything is happening, and this is probably just as well. The way we think at the unconscious level is usually complex and utterly foreign and confusing to our conscious mind.

Psychologists refer to this unconscious preparation and planning phase as an incubation period. During the incubation of an egg, the changes going on inside the egg from the time it is laid to when it is hatched are not visible to the outside world. So it is with the unconscious changes occurring within someone. Generally, the bigger the change, the longer the incubation period.

Even in the instance where a person seems to make a sudden and dramatic turnaround in their life, a sustained period of unconscious and invisible incubation has been taking place prior to the visible metamorphosis.

Support from Your Conscious Mind

Our conscious mind also has an important role to play during this time. At first it is more of a support role, providing your unconscious mind with the kind of environment it needs to pursue the goal of realizing your *intention*. This is accomplished by keeping the goal in your sights by consciously reaffirming your commitment to it. For some types of goals, such solving a complex mathematical problem, architecturally designing a new building, or writing a book, sustained conscious attention must be focused on the task at hand. To realize the intentions of most spells, however, extended conscious attention beyond what is called for in performing the ritual is not required and, as discussed below, can actually interfere.

There are a variety of approaches to consciously supporting the *intention* of a spell. Three examples are:

1. Regularly reminding yourself of your *intention* every evening before you go to bed. Simply reflect each evening on where you are and where you are going in relation to your goal.

2. Pick a specific time each day—for instance just before or after eating lunch—to reflect on your intention. Creating accurate images in your mind of how things will be different once your goal is accomplished can be part of this reflection.

3. You can write about your thoughts and reflections briefly each day in a journal or diary.[3]

Keep these periods of conscious reflection brief, and limit them to twice a day. It is important that you don't dwell on your *intention* throughout the day.

It is also necessary to be alert for signals from your unconscious that it is time to consciously take some action. Such signals can take many forms. At times your unconscious signals are more blatant and obviously connected with your *intention*. You may feel that you cannot postpone a certain action any longer, or the solution to some formerly intractable problem associated with your *intention* becomes obvious, or you may find that some task that you once found odious is tolerable or perhaps even pleasant. At other times it many seem as though these signals have nothing to do with your goal. You may get a certain urge to do something such as take a night course in some subject, or a thought could cross your mind to phone someone you haven't talked to for a long time, or you may wake up one morning just knowing it is time for you to move to a new house, or, for no reason you can identify, you vary your route to work in the morning.

You must also be alert for signals from the universe. How many opportunities for achieving your goal have presented themselves in the past and you haven't even recognized them or, if you did recognize them, you took no action? Now is the time to start recognizing opportunities and preparing for action. With your unconscious mind working diligently in the background to realize your *intention*, you will find this easier to do all the time.

---

3. Regularly writing in a journal is a very common practice among those who practice the magical arts. This discipline cannot be recommended enough, as it serves both as a valuable learning aid and personal reference. Many traditions refer to such a journal as a *Book of Shadows*.

Letting Go

Imagine what would happen if during the incubation of an egg the hen took a notion that the egg didn't know what it was doing and set about to help it. The hen might decide that rolling the egg around would provide it with necessary stimulation, or leaving it in the sunlight might warm it even more than sitting on it, or the hen may even decide to crack into the shell to see what's going on. The results, of course, would be disastrous and the chances of the egg successfully hatching would be slim.

The actions of this hen are analogous to what some people do with their conscious minds during the unconscious incubation period. They worry, scheme, rationalize, and engage in any number of activities both mental and physical that offer some illusion of conscious control. It is just an illusion. What they are actually doing is interfering. What such people must learn to do is to *let go*.

Letting go is a key principle in the psychology of realizing *intentions* and, as discussed in the next chapter, in the realm of magic as well. It is essential for successful incubation. To better understand this principle, it is useful to distinguish between letting go and ignoring something. Remember that the role of your conscious mind during the incubation phase is to let go of control, not to ignore your *intention*. Its job is to provide your unconscious mind with the support it needs to work. You do this by daily reaffirming your commitment to the *intention* and by being alert to signals from your unconscious and to the opportunities around you (and when appropriate, acting on them). Conscious support does not mean dwelling on the subject. In fact, except for the brief daily reaffirmations of your goal, going for days without consciously thinking about your *intention* can be very useful. For those of you who may have a difficult time letting go, just remember the brooding hen. The egg hatches most reliably when the hen provides it with the warmth it needs, keeps it out of harm's way and allows the magic of the egg to work. Nothing else the hen does will promote the egg to hatch, but it very well might interfere.

Recognizing a Realized Intention

Once your goal has been realized, at least to a certain extent, it is as if the egg has hatched. The hen must switch from the relative inactivity of brooding to caring for and feeding lively, animated chicks. From this point on the hen is very busy. Similarly, when you reach the point where your intention is beginning to be realized, it is the time for your conscious mind to become fully engaged and active.

As strange as it may seem, people sometimes don't recognize when they have reached their goal.[4] This is not at all uncommon and can happen for a variety of reasons. You may have arrived at your goal in such gradual steps that there was no clear threshold point. You may be so used to being on the road to your goal that you forget that there is a destination. Sometimes people start out not having a clear idea, or having the wrong idea, about what realizing their intention will be like.

Not recognizing that your intention is realized can lead to problems. It is analogous to our hen not realizing the eggs had hatched. If this happens, rather than varying her behavior and feeding her chicks, she will continue to sit on them as if they were still eggs. If this goes on long enough, then the chicks will not survive. Likewise, inaction on your part once your intention has been realized can see the results of your achievements being lost. Every now and then ask yourself the question, "Is it possible that my intention has been realized?" Consider your answer carefully. You may be in for a surprise.

Humor

Humor is not usually associated with either psychology or magic, as both pursuits are often viewed as austere, sober affairs. Magic in particular conjures images of very serious people engaged in somber and even melodramatic acts. When have you ever seen a picture of a laughing magician? Like all stereotypes, these notions are inaccurate and at the same time based upon some truth.

Many people who are practitioners of both magical and psychological disciplines take themselves very seriously and believe they are engaged in practices too important to be sullied with the baseness of humor. This is unfortunate, as taking ourselves or our circumstances too seriously is frequently a major contributor to our problems, and the best thing we can do is to find the humor in the situation. (See the spell Not Taking Yourself or Your Situation So Seriously in Part II, page 166.) Humor is an excellent tool for changing your perspective on something. Humor is also a powerful vehicle for both building and releasing psychic energy in casting some types of spells.

Of course there are situations where humor is not appropriate, such as when focused concentration is required, or if it is at someone else's expense, but common

---

4. What is even more remarkable is how often people long for what they already have. All that is required is that they recognize it.

sense is all that is needed to make this determination. In most applications, humor is a healing tonic and it deserves an honored place in both psychology and magic. Use it liberally.

Hypnotic Trance

Hypnotic trance is a subject about which there are many misconceptions, and in some circles there is considerable disagreement. As with other complex or controversial topics in *Foundations of Magic* our discussion of trance will be limited to what is useful for our purpose of working effective magic. Our operational definition of trance is as follows:

> **A state of alert relaxation and altered consciousness that facilitates greater ease of accepting suggestions, and allows more direct contact with the workings of our unconscious mind.**

As exotic as this may sound, trance is actually a natural and common experience into which we all enter, to varying degrees, many times a day. Spacing out, daydreaming, and being completely caught up in someone's story are all forms of trance. A hypnotist is someone who purposely leads other people into this natural state of trance, and by using suggestion deepens the trance and directs the subject's experience and sometimes their behavior. With self-hypnosis a person purposely leads himself or herself into trance, acting as both the hypnotist and subject. Self-hypnosis in order to achieve certain beneficial trance states is necessary for the preparation and ritual of some spells.

When using self-hypnosis it is sometimes an advantage to achieve a certain trance depth—light, medium, or deep—depending on the purpose of the exercise. The deeper someone is in trance, the less that person is in contact with their five senses and the outside world, and the more their reality is comprised of what is going on inside their head. Have you ever disturbed someone who was deep in thought and watched them have to shake their head or look around in order to orient themselves before they could respond to you? This behavior indicates a fairly deep level of spontaneous trance. Children who are completely involved in playing a video game or watching cartoons on television often evidence an even deeper level. They can become incapable of registering the fact that someone is talking to them and it can require a forceful intervention, such as turning off the set, to get their attention and end the trance state.[5] The procedures in Step 2, outlined on page 55, will provide you with a way to monitor your own trance depth.

Before proceeding with instructions for hypnotizing yourself, a few comments may be in order to address some commonly held concerns. Once you have succeeded in putting yourself in trance, you will not become vulnerable to other people's will. After all, it is you who is doing the hypnotizing. The self-induction outlined below is designed to be comfortable, relaxing, and free of unpleasant experiences. There is no way you can "get stuck" in trance. You are in control at all times. Even if for some reason everything were to go wrong, the worst that could happen is that you would fall asleep and wake up refreshed. Self-hypnosis is not at all difficult, but it is a learned skill. Some people have a natural affinity for it and slip easily and quickly into an intentional trance. Others take longer and can experience difficulties from the beginning. Regardless of your apparent aptitude, regular practice for a few days will ensure success. Familiarize yourself with the procedure outlined below and be conscientious about completing Exercise 6. You will not only develop the ability to intentionally enter into trance, but you will also benefit from the experience itself.

Self-Hypnosis

Setting Up

Find a place to practice your trance work where you will not be disturbed. Ideally this should be the same place where you plan to practice magic. If you are limited to doing this in a noisy environment, and you find the noise distracting, there are several things you can do. One simple solution that works for many people is to wear ear plugs. If this proves too uncomfortable or otherwise unsatisfactory, then masking the noise with some other less distracting noise, such as an electric fan, can be helpful. Background music can be used, but you must take care in your selection. Choose music that does not have any lyrics and does not create tension or evoke emotions. Some of the more subdued New Age background music can work well.

---

5. Strictly speaking, this should probably not be considered spontaneous self-hypnosis. The video game and television are actually acting as the hypnotist, which is a somewhat disquieting thought.

Once you become proficient in entering a hypnotic trance, use of sound insulating or masking devices should be phased out. If you continue to use them you will rely on them and they may inappropriately trigger you into trance if you encounter them in other contexts. Perhaps the best solution is to suggest to yourself just before you begin that you will soon forget about the noise and it will drift out of your consciousness. Later you can elaborate on this self-message to suggest that any loud noises will only assist you into going deeper into trance.

You will learn to induce trance while sitting or standing but especially if self-hypnosis is new to you, start by lying down on your back on a mat or thick carpet. Don't use a couch or bed, as these are too often a trigger for sleep. In the beginning, lying down is the easiest position from which to complete Step 1, Relax Your Entire Body. If you find that you begin to fall asleep, a problem for some beginners, sit up against a wall instead. If sleep is still an issue, switch to sitting in a hard chair and from there to sitting on the edge of a chair,[6] to finally standing up. If you fall asleep standing up, you are probably not getting nearly enough sleep and you should attend to this problem before proceeding.

Establishing a Gateway

The last consideration before you begin practicing your trance state is establishing a gateway for trance. Your gateway will involve two elements: words and a visual image. Each time, just before you begin Step 1, say to yourself, *"Now I enter the gateway to my inner self."* Make sure this is something you don't ever say to yourself in any other circumstances. Create a unique mental picture of your gateway. This image should literally portray a gate or door that opens as you say the gateway words. It does not have to be sustained for longer than it takes you to see it open at the beginning of your trance work. As with the gateway words, this mental picture should never be used for any other purpose. Saying your beginning words and conjuring this image is referred to as *entering the gateway* to trance. As you become more practiced your gateway can be used to very quickly get you into trance.

---

6. If you fall asleep sitting on the edge of a chair, you are probably not getting nearly enough sleep and you should attend to this problem before proceeding.

Steps to Self-Hypnosis

Read the following procedures several times before attempting to practice them. You must memorize the steps, as you cannot both read and follow these instructions at the same time. Memorize any italicized text word for word. When you feel ready to begin, look over the outline of the four steps in appendix 1 and make sure you know what each step involves.

Step 1. Relax Your Entire Body. This step consists of a standard technique, used in many applications, for relaxing your body. Begin by assuming your favored position and closing your eyes. Starting at your toes, become aware of each part of your body and as you do, consciously relax it. From your toes move on to the rest of your foot, then your ankle, then your lower legs, and then your calves, and so forth. Proceed gradually up your entire body, including your arms and hands, until you get to the top of your head. Take your time. Remember that this not about rushing to accomplish something; it is about relaxing.

Be particularly aware of releasing any tension in your jaw, shoulders, neck, genitals, and anus. These are common areas that need relaxing. There is a very simple and effective technique if you are having difficulty knowing what to do to relax a certain part of your body: Tense it tightly and then release it. When you release, be conscious of releasing completely.

Throughout this process you may be bothered with mental monkey chatter and random thoughts. Know that this is natural and that these experiences can simply be allowed to happen and ignored. Attempts to consciously stop these thoughts will be ineffective and are unnecessary.

Step 2. Travel Down. Enter the gateway by saying the words, "*Now I enter the gateway to my inner self.*" You are about to start a journey down into yourself. In order to do this, imagine that you pass through your gateway onto a psychic elevator. If you are uncomfortable in elevators, imagine that you are in a magic bubble or on a platform or some other imaginary device that can comfortably convey you. The elevator (or bubble or platform) is unusual in a number of ways. It has no walls, but is surrounded with a transparent force field that makes it open, roomy, warm, and very secure. It is pleasantly appointed and, all in all, it is a fine place to be. **Unlike other elevators, when you use this one, you always get on at the top floor and the floor numbers *increase* as**

you go down. There is a sign on the inside of the elevator that lists one of its special features.

> **"The deeper you go, the more relaxed and comfortable and alert you become, and the more capable you become of learning new things in new ways."**

Memorize the words on this sign and each time you begin to descend, recite them to yourself in your mind.

This is a completely self-service elevator, and you can stop it or reverse its direction any time you wish. This elevator is completely under your control. Begin by pushing the "down" button. Feel yourself slowly and smoothly being lowered into your own trance. You can hear a pleasant tone sound each time you pass a floor. There are ten floors and each floor you pass indicates you are deeper in your trance. Remind yourself that you are going slowly deeper into trance.

Your first few times on the elevator you may not even know what it means to go into trance. Nothing may feel any different. You may be on the lookout for what trance is like and be checking for different feelings. These sorts of reactions are normal. Tell yourself that, even if you don't know it or can't feel it, you are going into trance because your unconscious mind knows what it is and you can trust your unconscious mind.

Remind yourself that you can stop or reverse the direction of the elevator any time you wish. Continue to descend very slowly, hearing the tone at each floor you pass. The first time you do this exercise stop the elevator when you hear the tone for the third floor. Each day as you practice going into a trance you will descend a little further to the next floor down.

Once you have stopped, remain inside the comfort of the elevator (or bubble or platform) and take a look around at what there is to see outside. What do you see? What is the predominant color of the things outside the elevator? Stare at one location for a few moments and see what emerges into your field of vision. Remember this is not a test. You cannot fail at this. You can only succeed. Whatever you see or don't see is up to your unconscious, and that is what is important.

Step 3. Perform a Task. For each spell that requires self-hypnosis you will be asked to perform a certain task or follow a certain procedure while in trance. These are always tasks that are easier or more effective when performed in the trance state. For example, in Exercise 6, Practicing Self-Hypnosis, you are asked to make a series of suggestions to yourself and then to relax and re-energize yourself for a set length of time.

Step 4. Return from Trance. After you complete your task, push the "up" button and start your ascent out of trance (from here on this will be referred to as *ascending up out of trance*). You can control how fast the elevator rises. Memorize the following message so that, as you ascend, you can recite it in your mind as if it is being played over the elevator's public address system.

> **"As you ascend, you will find yourself more and more refreshed and alert with every floor you pass. When you reach the top you will be fully refreshed and alert."**

When you reach the top you will be completely out of trance. Open your eyes.

Streamlining

As you become more and more proficient at entering a self-induced trance, you will begin to streamline the process. For example, you will not have to lie down in order to obtain full-body relaxation (nor will you have to sit on the edge of a chair in order to prevent yourself from falling asleep, if you are one of the people for whom this is an issue). You will be able to relax and enter trance while assuming almost any body position. Eventually you can eliminate the entire visualization of the elevator. Just entering the gateway will allow you to very quickly and automatically go through all of the steps into whatever level of trance suits you. This is one reason you must never have your gateway triggers associated with any other activity.

Hypnosis is a great tool for personal development, and there are many hypnotic techniques that can be employed to effect many purposes. Anyone interested in finding out more about hypnosis can choose from the vast selection of books, tapes, and seminars available on the subject. For our purposes, use of self-hypnosis as described in the foregoing procedures is sufficient.

In order to be proficient at working spells, it is important that you become familiar with the process of self-inducing a trance state. Be conscientious about doing Exercise 6 below.

Practice the four steps of self-hypnosis once or twice every day for seven days. For this exercise, the task of Step 3, Perform a Task, is to make the following specific suggestions to yourself. Memorize these and say each one in your mind:

- Each day I practice the steps of self-hypnosis I will find it easier and easier to enter into trance.

- Each day I practice the steps of self-hypnosis I will find it easier and easier to control continually deeper trances.

- Each outside noise I hear during this exercise will assist me to go more easily into trance.

- Each day that I practice self-hypnosis a door will be opened to new possibilities and realizations that will benefit me.

The next suggestion will help you learn to control the specific time you are in trance, as well as provide physical and mental advantages for the rest of the day.

For the next five minutes I will remain in this state of trance to allow my mind and body to be rested and re-energized.

As you become more practiced, you can vary the time period or even allow your unconscious to decide how long it needs to rest and re-energize.

Most people will start to realize after a few days that they are indeed entering a trance. Although this realization can occur during the trance state it often does not, at least at first. Rather, it becomes apparent afterward, upon coming out of trance. If you find that you are persistently having difficulty with one or more of these steps, then turn to the *Law of Pretending* and *pretend* that you are doing everything exactly right. *Pretend* that your proficiency is increasing each time you practice. When you become familiar with the process, experiment with streamlining. Experiment with inducing a trance state by simply sitting down and *entering the gateway*. If at the end of seven days you do not believe that you have learned to go into a self-induced trance, then do the following. Go through the four steps to self-hypnosis one more time, except when you get to Step 3 do *not* give yourself the suggestions outlined above. Instead memorize and use the following suggestion.

> **"In the next 72 hours I will see something purple, which will safely and suddenly trigger in me a full realization that I have learned to go into trance."**

See what happens.

Higher States

Remember for a moment our definition of trance. Trance is "a state of alert relaxation and altered consciousness that facilitates greater ease of accepting suggestions and allows more direct contact with the workings of our unconscious mind." The *higher states* are a special case of trance, and for our purposes can be defined as follows:

> **A state of altered consciousness characterized by a heightened awareness of both your *higher self* and an increased ability to direct *your Will* to a purpose.**

In other words, it is the optimum state from which to work most magic. For most spells, just after you cast and cleanse your magic circle, you will be instructed to ascend to a *higher state*. Once you have become proficient at self-hypnosis, ascending to a *higher state* is simple. Just follow the instructions below, **but not before becoming capable of self-inducing a trance state.** Once you know how to intentionally enter into a trance, your unconscious mind will make perfect sense of the instructions for entering a *higher state*.

Before you begin, envision a second *gateway* that is completely different from the gateway for entering trance. Create a mental image of this gateway, distinct from your trance gateway image. The gateway words are, of course, different from those used for going into trance. Say, "***Now the gateway to my higher self opens.***" Saying the words and visualizing this gateway opening is referred to as *entering the gateway to your higher state.*

The steps for entering into a *higher state* are as follows.

Step 1. Enter into Trance. Follow the procedures for going into a medium trance and descend to the fourth or fifth floor level.

Step 2. Enter the *Gate way* to your *Higher State*. Say the words, "*Now the gateway to my higher self opens*," and visualize the gate opening.

Step 3. Ascend. Start the slow ascent up, being aware of when you are at the third level, and then the second, and then the first level. Instead of stopping and leaving trance as you have in the past, continue on up past the first floor. Be very aware that you are moving up and beyond the place where you began.

Step 4. Break Through and Experience Your *Higher State*. At some point in your slow ascent past the first floor, visualize that you break through into a completely different realm. You may imagine it as passing out through the roof of a building, or emerging from clouds or fog, or penetrating some ethereal membrane. Stop the elevator here and open your eyes, if they are not already open. It is here that you can begin to fully realize your *higher self*, your *true nature*. Around you is the universe, viewed with high vision and high energy. Be aware of your surroundings and of how you feel. You do not need to understand this place with your mind, rather you must experience it directly as you would the beauty in a flower, or the heat of the sun or the feeling of a longed-for kiss. Each time you come to this place you will, in the truest sense, understand it more. This is a place to be entered only from within your magic circle and from this place you can work the most marvelous magic. This place is not the only *higher state*. There are others. If you continue to practice magic for long you will discover these on your own or you will be led to them. To work the magic in *Foundations of Magic*, knowing how to arrive at this particular *higher state* is quite sufficient.

Step 5. Descend from your *Higher State*. When you have completed your work in your *higher state*, use your elevator to go back down to the top floor (your starting point). This descent will be referred to in the remainder of this book as *descending from your higher state*. Remind yourself that you are returning to your *un*altered state, refreshed and fully alert.

Streamlining

This is similar to the process of streamlining a trance induction. As you become proficient at ascending to your *higher state*, you can eliminate the need to first descend into trance. With time and practice you can enter your *higher state* by simply *entering the gateway to your higher state*.

EXERCISE 7   PRACTICE ASCENDING TO A HIGHER STATE

After you have become familiar with inducing your own trance state, practice the five steps of ascending to a *higher state*. Practice this once or twice a day for five days. For ready reference there is an outline of all five steps in appendix 1. Once you become proficient, practice streamlining. In other words, enter your *higher state* by *entering the gateway to your higher state* without first having to go into trance.

3

CASTING SPELLS

There are six basic stages in casting an effective spell. They are: *Designing a Well-Formed Intention, Rehearsal, Self-Preparation, Physical Preparations, Ritual,* and *Follow-up.* This chapter provides explanations and instructions for each stage, along with an exercise designed to give you firsthand experience at casting a spell. It also includes a brief but important discussion on the ethics of casting spells, along with some suggestions about what to do if a spell doesn't seem to be effective.

The Preparation Stages

In general, more time is required preparing for a spell than actually conducting the ritual. Four of the six stages are preparation stages. *Designing a Well-Formed Intention* and *Rehearsal* are two preparation stages that must be completed in essentially the same manner for every spell, and even though the *intention* and the rehearsed ritual are different each time, the specific instructions for these stages do not vary. On the other hand, the *Physical Preparations* and *Self-Preparation* instructions are different for each spell. Sometimes the procedures are lengthy and quite involved, and other times they are brief and simple, but they are always important. Working a spell without the proper attention to each preparation stage is a waste of time and energy, as a favorable outcome is unlikely.

Designing a Well-Formed Intention

It's obvious that before you work a spell you must have some *intention* about what you wish to accomplish. What is not always so obvious is whether or not the *intention* is the right one for you or the person for whom you are working the spell. In magic, the road to hell is not paved with good *intentions*, it's paved with poorly formed *intentions*.

Here are two examples of how problems can arise. Imagine for moment a single parent—we'll call him Jim—who is struggling to raise a child by himself. In our first example, Jim has come to the conclusion that the root of his struggle as a single parent is financial and that the best way to eliminate his struggle would be to have more money. He therefore forms an *intention* to work a spell to that purpose. If, however, Jim is a disaster at managing money, then he may find that having more money does not relieve his financial troubles. In this case he has simply formed the wrong *intention*. He would have benefited much more if he formed the *intention* to improve his money-managing skills.

Now let's assume, for our second example, that Jim is a competent money manager and simply needs more money on a regular basis. He forms an *intention* to regularly receive more money, and works a spell to that effect. A week after working the spell Jim picks up his monthly paycheck, which has a note attached explaining that due to higher company profits each employee will be receiving an extra twenty dollars a month for the next year. For Jim this extra income is not enough. He did not make it clear in his *intention* how much extra money he required.

There are any number of other examples of problems that can arise from working a spell when the *intention* of the spell is not well formed. The various considerations discussed below are important for sound *intention* design, and will help minimize or eliminate such problems. In appendix 2 you will find an *intention* design checklist that incorporates these considerations.

Choose the Right Intention

Working on the wrong *intention* is the mistake Jim made in the first example above. Determining whether or not an *intention* is the right one is the most basic consideration when forming an *intention*. If your *intention* is realized, will it accomplish what you want? Will it really solve your problem or improve your situation in the way you imagine it will? Perhaps the best way to check this out is to engage in a short fantasy game that psychologists sometimes refer to as "future pacing." Visualize a future time when your *intention* is fully realized. Make the experience as real as you can. Consider the details of your life from the perspective of having your *intention* actualized. Is your situation changed in the way you wanted it to be? Do any new problems arise now that you have succeeded in achieving your purpose? From the perspective of this imaginary future you can often gain insights into ways your *intention* should be changed.

Another method for checking if your *intention* is the right one is to talk about it with someone you trust and whose judgment you respect. Other people can often see what our own blind spots prevent us from seeing.

Be Free of Reservations and Doubts

What you intend should always be something about which you have no reservations. You must want and approve of your *intention* 100 percent in body, mind and spirit. If you don't, this is an indication of internal conflict. The part of you that is holding back is not in alignment with those parts of you that have formed the *intention*. In other words, some aspect of your *true nature* is not being acknowledged. If you proceed in this conflicted state you will be working toward something that is not completely right for you. You will also be missing the power of *Will*, as your *intention* will not be in harmony with your *true nature*. Never ignore your doubts; they are a signal that something needs to be changed. It could be that the *intention* is the wrong one for you. It may be that your *intention* is basically the right one but that something needs to be added or some aspect of it eliminated. Again consider our single parent, Jim. Rather than seeing financial matters at the root of his problem, he decides that being single is the problem and accordingly forms the *intention* to fall in love and be married and in a long-term stable relationship within a year. Shortly after forming this *intention* he starts having doubts. Upon reflection he realizes that what is nagging at him is the thought that whomever he marries may not love his child. He could then add this provision to his *intention*. Alternatively, he may realize that for some reason he needs to remove something, such as the provision about marrying within a year.

When reflecting on your *intention,* it is essential that you separate your doubts about your *intention* from uncertainties about the future. For example, Jim may feel concerns about marriage because he doesn't know exactly what is going to happen when he gets married. Will he be hurt as he was in the past? Will he stay in love with her or she with him? Will they fight? What if she becomes seriously ill or even dies? What if the marriage is a disaster in ways he can't even imagine from here? These questions have more to do with the realization that life is filled with uncertainties than they do with doubts about the *intention*. It is a law of nature that any course in life is filled with much uncertainty and even the strongest magic in the world can't change that. You can always try to reduce some specific uncertainties by addressing them in your *intention*. Past a certain point, however, adding addendums or codicils to your *intentions* starts to become an attempt to live your future life now. The question Jim needs to ask himself is this: "Am I willing to accept the uncertainties and risks that come with marriage?" If the answer is no, then this is not an *intention* that Jim can support 100 percent. If the answer is yes, then he can still have questions about how the future will turn out without doubting his *intention*.

Keep It Possible

Remember that magic works in harmony with the laws of nature, not counter to them. Remember to limit your *intentions* to those things that the laws of nature permit. For example, don't have the *intention* of walking through solid walls without the benefit of a doorway.[1]

Keep It Probable

If you have no money, but have the *intention* of being able to accumulate a certain amount of money within a year, specify an amount that is probable according to your circumstances. For example, for a person of average financial means, the *intention* to accumulate $5,000 within a year has a high degree of probability. If their goal is to accumulate $50,000 within a year, the probability is lowered considerably. If, however, their *intention* is to accumulate a million dollars within a year, the probability is quite small.

There are a couple of reasons why it is best to keep your *intentions* within the realm of what is probable. Perhaps the biggest issue with an improbable *intention* is that for most people it is difficult to accept 100 percent that it can be realized. Usually some part of our conscious or unconscious mind starts objecting when we enter the realm

---

1. The principles of quantum mechanics actually allow for the possibility of passing through walls, but the probability of it happening is exceedingly small. So small, in fact, that such an event is likely to happen only once in several million times the present age of the universe. This is probably too long to wait.

of high improbability, and that part of us can easily undermine such an *intention*. Another factor affecting such *intentions* is the sheer immensity of the forces that are required to realize them. There are no apparent laws of nature that are violated if someone who has no money accumulates a million dollars within a year, but the forces that must be put into play to see that this happens are enormous. This can require very strong magic indeed, and can be beyond the limit of our range of abilities.

Size the Task Appropriately

There may be a time in a person's life when going in pursuit of a seemingly unlikely goal is desirable or even necessary. Often this task can be made easier if it's broken into smaller tasks. For example, your first *intention* could be to accumulate $5,000 within the next two months. With this accomplished, you could next intend to double the money within the following two months and so on. This does not mean that starting from no money and accumulating a million dollars is easy, but it does mean the accomplishment of each *intention* along each step of the way is considerably more probable and therefore its realization by the use of magic is also easier.

Be Precise

In the second example, our single parent Jim was not precise about how much extra money he needed on a regular basis. He could have done this in several ways. He could have intended that his income increase by a specific amount each month, for instance $500, or he could have specified that specific financial criteria be met, for example, that his income increase to a level where he could meet all of his current living expenses plus enough additional money to allow him to buy a new car within a year. In some ways the working of an *intention* is similar to a legal document. The particulars should be spelled out as clearly and completely as is feasible. As discussed below in Identify the Essence, however, this is not always practical, particularly with large systemic changes.

Be Literal

Be sure you can state your *intention* in plain, simple language. The use of colorful expressions, metaphor, and simile are important parts of lively, expressive speaking and writing, but they can be disastrous in forming *intentions* for the purpose of working a spell. If you are forming an *intention* to acquire more money state it plainly and ask for money, not bucks, greenbacks, or bread, or you could become inundated with male deer, or lizards, or unexpectedly inherit a bakery. If you are working on some aspect of your own personal development, then avoid using terms such as personal growth or expanding your horizons, or you could end up gaining weight or moving to the prairies. This may sound like a joke, and it is. It's a cosmic joke, which as many have experienced, can be played on you if your language is at all ambiguous due to metaphor.

Organ language is a particular category of metaphor that can be especially troublesome. Organ language includes expressions that refer to parts of the body but are not intended to be taken literally; for example, "He gives me a pain in the neck," "All you do is bellyache," or "It just breaks my heart." The use of organ language in working spells, as well as repeated use in everyday conversation, can lead to the affliction described in the metaphor.

Common expressions and metaphors are such a part of our normal speech patterns that it can be difficult to recognize them. When you believe you have completely formed your *intention,* write it down. Then take a moment to check each word you have written and ask yourself if you are using the word literally or metaphorically. Be sure that the *intention* that you finally use is a literal statement.

Much of the language found in the spells seems to run counter to this advice because it is often quite metaphorical in nature. It is important to distinguish between the wording of the *intention* and the wording of the spell itself. What we are addressing in this chapter is the formation of your *intentions,* so that when the magic works it works to your purpose. The words incorporated into the ritual of the spell itself are part of the means by which that *intention* is realized.

State It Positively

Whenever you are using words to indicate your *intentions* or desires it is best to make a positive statement. This does not necessarily mean making an upbeat statement, just don't make a statement using "not," "will not," "don't," or other negating words. The first sentence in this paragraph is a positive statement. The second is a negative statement. There are two problems with *intentions* formed with negative statements. They often convey information about what you want to avoid, but little or no information about what you wish to accomplish. They can also force your unconscious mind to consider the very thing you are attempting to avoid. Here is a trivial example. If you want a friend to choose red wallpaper for their bedroom but you are concerned that they may choose blue, you can state your desire in either the positive or the negative. If you make a positive statement such as "choose red," you are being clear about what you want. If instead you say, "don't choose blue," you give no information about which color you prefer. In addition, your friend's mind must consider "blue," exactly what you are trying to avoid, before it can even make any meaning out of the sentence.

Occasionally, stating things in the positive can be tricky. For instance, if you wish to stop smoking, almost any way you attempt to accurately express this in words requires verbally negating the act of smoking (I will be smoke-free, I will refrain from using cigarettes, I will be an ex-smoker, I quit). If you must state an *intention* as a negation end the statement with a positive statement and make positive images of your *intention*. For example, you may form your *intention* something like this: "I intend to become a nonsmoker and improve my health and well-being." You can then make a series of images of yourself relaxed, contented, and healthy in various situations where in the past you would have wanted a cigarette.

Identify the Essence

An alternative strategy to being accurate about the details of your *intention* is to be accurate about the essence of what you want. This is the best approach to complex or systemic changes when you are working with insufficient information. For instance, in a family where tension and conflict are common, a person may have the *intention* of bringing harmony to the family. It would be extremely difficult in this situation to be precise or accurate about how each family member's behavior and relationship to other members should change in order for this to come about. This type of systemic change is best approached by formulating an *intention* that captures the **essence** of the change you want. In this case your stated *intention* will specify the criteria of your goal in broader terms. For instance, an *intention* for bringing harmony to a family could be stated as follows:

> **"Let the five members of my immediate family live together in ever-increasing harmony, so that within a year conflict is rare and tolerance, appreciation, and enjoyment of each other is common."**

This is a well-stated *intention,* but it leaves open many possibilities for how such a set of criteria could be met. To exaggerate the point, consider a situation in which all five family members become heroin addicts and within a year find themselves all regularly sitting around the house shooting up and enjoying each other very much indeed. This, strictly speaking, would meet the conditions of the *intention* as stated. To prevent such cosmic misunderstandings, this *intention* needs to contain more information than exists in the stated form. This is where your feelings and imagination can play a major role. What would it feel like to live with your family if there were more harmony? What would it look like?

Get in Touch with How It Would Feel

If you can get in touch with what it feels like to live in a relatively harmonious family (what family is completely harmonious?) then you have identified a very basic component of the essence of your *intention*. This tends to shift the emphasis from other people to you. After all, this is **your** feeling that you are talking about, and any way you come to have this feeling, regardless of what other people do, will satisfy your *intention*. Generally, even with major or complex changes, your *intention* is best defined by more than just a feeling. This is where your ability to make mental images is most useful.

Create Accurate Images

It is essential to have a good, clear image or series of images of what things would look like once your *intention* has been realized. This is true even if you have a simple and precisely worded *intention*. Some of the same criteria that apply to the wording of an *intention* need to be considered when forming an image of your *intention*: keep it possible, favor what is more probable, and be accurate. If you cannot consciously make clear mental images, then invoke the *Law of Pretending* and *pretend* that you can. *Pretend* that all of the elements that describe your *intention* are in the image.

Write It Down

When you have chosen the way in which you wish to state your *intention*, write it down. Read what you have written and ask yourself if it adequately expresses your *intention*. If necessary, edit it to more clearly reflect your true *intention*. This written statement will assist you in memorizing the verbal portion of your *intention*, and it will be a record for you to reflect upon later as you assess the effectiveness of the spell you cast.

Rehearsal

When you are casting a spell it is important that your concentration be on the *intention* of the spell and exercising your *Will*, not on trying to figure out what you should do or say next. In many ways a spell should be performed very much like a stage play. The smoother and more seamless the performance, the better the response. To achieve this smoothness, practice and rehearsal of the *Ritual* stage are essential. There are three steps to rehearsing a spell:

1. Learn the actual *Ritual* procedure by reading it over, walking through it and memorizing what you are supposed to do and in what order. When you believe that you have familiarized yourself enough, read over the **bold headings** in the *Ritual* stage and confirm that you know what they refer to in detail. These headings are intended to be used as memory cues when casting your spell.

2. Learn those words that are intended to be spoken from memory. They are separated from the body of instructional text and ***are marked out in bold italics.*** Rehearse them until you can recite them easily and smoothly from memory.

3. Some of the words are intended to be read out loud rather than spoken from memory. Again, they are separated from the body of instructional text but **they are printed in bold text that is *not* italicized.** Familiarize yourself with them so that you can read them fluidly.

Self-Preparation

The *Self-Preparation* stage of each spell includes procedures and exercises intended to prepare you psychologically for working the spell. For each spell there is a set of *Self-Preparation* instructions that you are to follow much as you might follow a recipe in a cookbook. The skills and techniques required to follow these instructions have been discussed at length in chapter 2 and need not be elaborated upon here. Remember the metaphor of fertile soil and barren soil at the beginning of chapter 2 and be thorough in your *Self-Preparation*.

Physical Preparations

All spells require preparation of your working space. Many call for the preparation of certain implements, substances, or symbols. Specific instructions for these things are given for each spell. In addition to these specific instructions, the following general considerations must be addressed for every spell.

Location

A location where you can work undisturbed is required for the practice of magic. If you live in a particularly warm, dry climate, this could be outdoors, but in many cases this will be an indoor space. If possible use the same location every time. Although rarely available to most people, it is ideal to have a place that is only used for this purpose.

As discussed in detail below, casting a magic circle is an essential part of the ritual for each spell, and therefore the working space should be large enough to allow free movement within a circle seven-to-nine feet in diameter. Outside noises should be minimal and the acoustic characteristics should be such that you can speak in a loud voice without disturbing people outside the space. A less tangible but equally important criterion is that the space be a pleasant one, or at least one that you can decorate in a pleasing manner.

Purification of Articles & Elements

Many of the items and substances that are brought into the circle as part of the ritual are invariably associated with mundane purposes. Basil, water, a dish, matches, and a mirror, for example, are used in one or more of the spells in *Foundations of Magic*. Each one of these common items has a myriad of associations with our daily life, and must be freed of these associations and influences. Purification is the formal act of dedicating these things to the higher purpose of working magic and pronouncing them free, at least temporarily, of their connection with the mundane. This is accomplished by performing a simple ceremony that is akin to the cleansing ritual described on page 78. This ceremony can be enacted at any time before you begin the actual ritual of casting a spell. Just be certain that none of the purified items or materials is used for mundane purposes in the meantime.

Place all of the items that you wish to purify in front of you, displayed so that each article and substance is clearly visible. Hold each individual item in your gaze and, as you do, say the words:

"I dedicate this [name of article or element] to a higher purpose of Will and cleanse it from all past associations and influences of the mundane."

As you speak these words, use your imagination to visualize the evaporation of the mundane associations, connections, and influences that had attached themselves to the item. Hold your gaze until your imagination sees the item clear and free of any vapors from the past.

Items that are to be stored and used exclusively for working spells need be purified only once. When practical, such items should be stored together in a location reserved for the purpose. For example, some people use a small bedside table as the working surface for their ritual. Smaller articles are kept inside the table drawer or shelf, and the table and its contents are always put away in the same place.[2] Items that are put back to everyday use need to be purified each time they are used again in a spell. Each item returned to daily use should be put away with care and with a quiet acknowledgment of its role in your spell.

Clothing & Jewelry

Whenever possible, the clothes that are worn for performing a ritual should be reserved for that purpose alone. They should always be made from natural materials. Wear cotton, linen, or wool. Silk, although natural, is considered a psychic and magic insulator and its use in ritual clothing should be avoided, at least by beginners. Synthetic fabrics are not suitable. Clothing should be warm, loose-fitting, comfortable, and unique.[3] It is best to remove your shoes and work a spell in bare feet or socks. Donning specially reserved garments that have a distinctive appearance and feel is a

---

2. Silk is an insulator of forces both magical and mundane. This makes it ideal for protecting your articles of magic from unwanted influences. On the other hand, its insulating property renders it inappropriate as a wrapping for charms, talismans, or other articles where the intention is to increase or channel various magical influences. Ideally, when not in use, all of the items reserved exclusively for working magic should be wrapped in silk cloth of any color but black. Do not be concerned, however, if you cannot get silk for this purpose, as your purification rite and thoughtful care in storing your articles is, in all but rare instances, more than sufficient.

3. There are some practitioners of magic who wear a tight-fitting belt or other restrictive item for protection from negative entities. Its very restrictiveness is designed to continually remind the magician of this function. This practice is often associated with rituals of evocation and is not appropriate for *Foundations of Magic*.

very powerful way to signal to yourself and the universe that magic is about to be worked.[4] The same applies to jewelry, such as an amulet, which is reserved exclusively for working magic.

It is best if you remove your everyday jewelry before entering the circle. This again is a way of marking out the line between ordinary time and space and magical time and space. If you have jewelry that you normally leave on all the time and do not wish to remove for the ritual, then use it to your advantage as a *bridge* symbol. To do this, either directly or with a mirror, gaze at it and say the following words.

> **"Let this [name of object] be the bridge between inner and outer and may it keep securely confined within its own physical boundaries the influences of both."**

Although a *bridge* symbol is not necessary, it can be helpful. Touching the piece of jewelry with your fingers in the moment just before entering or leaving the magic circle can provide a bridge for an easier transition between the two realities.

Using This Book

Foundations of Magic is itself a special *bridge symbol* as it contains both the mundane and the magical. Before using this book in the ritual of casting a spell, purify it by saying the following words:

> **"Let this book be the bridge between inner and outer and between the mundane and the magical, and may it keep securely confined within its own physical boundaries the influences of both."**

Always treat *Foundations of Magic* with care and respect. It is your touchstone while you are in your magic circle (see page 76), and the source from which you will read words of power.

---

4. Followers of some Pagan traditions often prefer to perform their rituals without clothes. If this appeals to you then by all means try it, but ensure that your nudity does not distract you from the work at hand, either due to self-consciousness or because you find it chilly.

The Working Surface

A working surface or *stand* inside the circle is needed for most spells, to provide a place to put things. Even those rituals that don't specifically call for the use of implements or other material require the use of a vessel for cleansing. As most magic is worked standing up, a flat surface elevated off the floor is essential. This surface, referred to here as a *stand,* and often referred to as an altar in magic parlance, should be positioned in the center of the circle. A small nightstand is ideal for most people. A nightstand not only provides a working surface, it usually incorporates a drawer or shelf space in which to store other items regularly used for magic. Occasionally, as when you are required to read from *Foundations of Magic* while it is open on the working surface, you may need to elevate the nightstand by placing it on a box or other suitable platform. A book holder, such as those commonly used for cookbooks, can be useful for keeping *Foundations of Magic* open to the proper page.

As mentioned above, magic should be worked in pleasant surroundings. If the *stand* is not an attractive piece of furniture, then cover it with decorative cloth. A candle in a pleasing candleholder can provide light for the ritual as well as improve the overall ambiance. Incidentally, never use an electric lamp inside your circle. Dimmed electric light elsewhere in the room is acceptable, but even then candlelight or light from an oil lamp is preferable. Always be sure to take the proper fire safety precautions when using candles or other open flames.

When enacting a ritual, unless otherwise instructed, you will face the *stand.* If, for example, you are directed to face East, then position yourself on the West side of the *stand* looking across it to the East. Even though the working surface is usually placed at the geometric center of the magic circle, it is important to remember that *you* are always at the true center, for it is by your magic that the circle is cast.

Ritual

The *Ritual* stage is the heart of any spell. It is during this stage that the person casting a spell enters magical time and space and projects their *Will* to the purpose at hand. This is a time of drama, when the influences of magical forces, ceremony, and a prepared psyche converge to bring about change in the world.

Centering Yourself

Before proceeding with any ritual it is beneficial to become centered. There is nothing mysterious or complex about the idea or the practice. "Gathering your wits about you" or "collecting yourself" are two old-fashioned ways of describing becoming centered. There are countless ways to center yourself, and if you have a favorite method that works for you, by all means use it. If not, follow this simple procedure:

- Whether standing or sitting, place both feet firmly on the ground.

- Become aware of your breathing.

- Allow yourself to breathe regularly and deeply, breathing in through your nose and out through your mouth.

- Concentrate on the sensation of air entering your lungs on the inhalation and leaving your body on the exhalation.

- With each exhalation, imagine expelling any busy thoughts, concerns, or tension.

Continue this for a few minutes until you feel composed.

Casting a Magic Circle

The magic circle defines the physical area in which rituals are performed, and is one of the more important elements in ceremonial magic.[5] From the point of view of our everyday experience, it is an imaginary circle created in the mind of the magician. From the magical and psychic perspective, however, there is nothing imaginary about it. This very difference in perception reflects the circle's primary function—to separate inner reality from outer reality. It defines the boundary between magical space and mundane space, between the domain of consciousness necessary to direct *Will* to a purpose and the domain of everyday consciousness. The magic circle provides protective sanctuary where ritual is normal and magic assumed.

To begin, stand facing east with your right arm extended and your index finger pointing outward. Imagine a blue-white stream of energy entering your body. Practitioners of various schools of magic differ as to where they experience the source of

---

5. Variations of the magic circle are central to many magical, mystical, and religious practices worldwide.

this energy. Some have it originating from the cosmos directly above and entering through the top of their head. Others have it flowing into them through their nose as they breath in or entering through "one point," which is a spot a couple of inches below the navel. Trust your own intuition on this and visualize what seems right to you. If you have no sense of the source and entry point of this energy then allow your unconscious mind to take over and make one up. Once the stream of energy has entered your body, imagine it flowing to the area of your heart and then down your arm and out your finger. What is important is an awareness that this magical energy flows through you.

Slowly turn clockwise, envisioning the energy stream marking out the perimeter of a circle with yourself at the center.[6] Make sure you cast the circle a full 360 degrees so that the ends connect and the circle is closed. It is a matter of individual preference where you imagine the circle being cast. You can visualize it materializing in the air, level with your heart or level with your center of gravity ("one point") or, as some prefer, on the ground.[7] This circle actually defines a three-dimensional space within which to cast a spell. The geometry of the 3-D space is also a matter of personal choice. It can be seen as a clear sphere or egg-shaped bubble with the circle as its diameter, or as a column extending infinitely above and below you. What is important here is that you clearly imagine the three dimensional boundary of the space created within the circle.

In general the size of the circle will depend on what is to be included inside it. If you are including a *stand* as a working surface then the circle should be large enough to allow you to move freely around it and still remain within the circle. If you are working without a *stand*, then the circle can be somewhat smaller. On occasion, as in the spell Attracting Money, Long Term (page 138), an entire house or other large area may be included.

As you are casting your circle, say the following words:

---

6. The terms *sunwise* or *deosil*, meaning "in the direction the sun moves," are often used in place of the word "clockwise" when discussing magic. Similarly, the word *widdershins*, meaning "counter to the direction the sun moves," is used instead of "counterclockwise." These terms are not used here in an effort to avoid unnecessary jargon.

7. Older pictures of magicians working magic often show them standing on a circle that is inlaid or otherwise drawn onto the floor. The circle is usually embellished with various symbols and designs. For our purposes this is unnecessary and even undesirable, as an important part of the *Ritual* is both casting and dispersing the circle. The rigid definition of a permanent circle can interfere with this process.

"Let this circle mark the boundary between the magical and the mundane, and within its perimeter let there be true sanctuary where nothing may enter except that I Will it so."

Remember that every word you utter, everything that your body is doing, and every physical prop you use in a ritual is directed toward providing your mind with the structure it needs to work magic. When you are turning and casting your circle, focus your mind on the task. Use your imagination to see the circle's boundaries. Be conscious of the feeling inside the circle once it is completed. Remind yourself that within your circle you are at the very center of the universe. You *are* the center of the universe. In your imagination actively be aware that you are in a sanctuary, a special protected place where inner calmness and exhilaration can coexist simultaneously and where magic happens. Become aware of the ways, both subtle and obvious, in which you are different inside this sacred space.

Of final importance is the following injunction: Once you have *cast your circle,* never break it by passing though it or by allowing anyone else to pass through it. Always *disperse the circle* (see page 80) before leaving the space, or allowing the space to be used for other purposes.

Cleansing Your Circle

Cleansing or purification is the process of eliminating any residue of conflicting, chaotic, or negative forces that may be left over from everyday activities. Upon completion of the cleansing ritual, your circle encompasses pure magical space, unencumbered by mundane influences. There may be a tendency to skimp on this step and not perform this part of the ritual with complete involvement. The cleansing process would not be included here if it were not just as important and indispensable as the rest of the circle ritual. Committed, conscious participation is required.

A variety of substances can be used for ritual cleansing, but one of the simplest is a rosemary tea made with clean, natural spring or creek water. If you cannot get clean water directly from its source then buy bottled spring water. Tap water should be avoided unless absolutely necessary. Rosemary has a long tradition of possessing purification powers. A quantity of this tea can be made in advance by steeping two teaspoons of fresh or dried (not ground or powdered) rosemary in a quart of boiling water and allowing it to cool to room temperature. Strain the tea and store it in the refrigerator.

Before you begin your ritual, pour a cup or so of the tea into a ceramic, glass, or metal container, preferably a chalice or goblet. Plastic containers are not suitable. Start cleansing your circle by holding the tea vessel in your left hand and facing east. Dip the fingers of your right hand in the tea and with a flicking motion sprinkle tea toward the east three times. As you do this, say the words:

> **"With the power of this herb of the Sun and the purity of this water, I cleanse the eastern domain."**

Turn clockwise and repeat this procedure facing each of the remaining cardinal directions (saying the name of the appropriate direction each time). Visualize the space within the circle's boundaries becoming clear and free of all outside connections and influences. As you become more practiced at this, you will find that the appearance of the very air within the circle takes on a palpably different visual quality.

Proclaiming Your Intention

This is a pivotal step in working magic. Here is where you proclaim to yourself and the universe your carefully designed *intention* and state the purpose for working the spell. The rest of the ritual of casting the spell is directed toward the realization of this *intention*. Start by saying the following words:

> **"This ritual is well and truly commenced to accomplish the purpose of my Will, which I proclaim to be as follows . . ."**

Make sure you have memorized the final written version of your *intention* and state it fully in a firm clear voice. Bring into your mind the mental images of what your *intention* will look like once it is realized. As you do these things, connect with any feelings that will accompany the fulfillment of your *intention*.

Casting Your Spell

Once you have proclaimed your intention, you can commence with the remainder of the ritual of casting a particular spell. This usually, but not always, begins with ascending to a *higher state* and ends by descending from a *higher state*. The particular instructions for each spell are given in Part II. Enact the ceremony as you have rehearsed it. Be completely focused.

Unless indicated otherwise, all of the words of a spell are to be spoken out loud. The instructions for each spell will indicate the manner in which to speak. Sometimes you will be instructed to speak loudly and with force and other times calmly with quiet purpose. Some spells use the Wiccan principle of slowly building and then suddenly releasing psychic energy. When casting such a spell the tone, tempo, and volume of your voice will need to vary, corresponding to the intensity of the building energy. In every case you will be required to speak with conviction and confidence. Again, if you have any difficulty with realizing the desired speaking style, invoke the *Law of Pretending* and, with focused intent, act as if you are speaking exactly the way you need to be.

When reading from *Foundations of Magic*, either hold the book open in one hand, leaving the other hand free, or alternatively, have it open on the stand where it is easy to read. Connect with the spoken words of a spell in the same way that an actor would with the words of a script, or that a poet would reciting their own poetry. It is you who is using these words of power; let them come from you.

Dispersing Your Circle

When your ritual has concluded, it is important that you disperse the circle. Once again, the intention is to clearly mark out the transition from magical space back to ordinary space. This procedure must be performed with the same conscious attention and focus that was used in casting your circle, but this time use the index finger of your left hand to erase the circle. Face east and turn slowly counterclockwise, allowing the energy of the circle to be reabsorbed into you. As the energy enters your body, be aware that it is being assimilated as vital energy and is permeating every fiber of your being to charge and ready you for your revitalized return to the everyday. As you do this say the words:

> **"My work here is well and truly completed, and the circle is dispersed until further needed."**

Visualize the circle disappearing and the boundaries of the magical space fading until you have eradicated the entire circle.

Follow-up

Some spells require that certain procedures are followed after you have completed the *Ritual*. This follow-up phase is an essential part of casting your spell, and deserves to be implemented with the same conscientiousness as each of the other phases.

EXERCISE 8   A PRACTICE SPELL

This exercise is intended to familiarize you with the procedures of casting a spell and the experience of being in magical space. Once you are set up, it should take no more than about 15 or 20 minutes. Practice it once a day for three or four days in row.

Stage 1. Designing a Well-Formed Intention
For the purposes of this exercise your *intention* is to become familiar with the magical space inside a magic circle. You can state this as an *intention* "to experience magical space and to **learn** about the magic within this circle which I have cast and to claim its sanctuary as mine."

Stage 2. Rehearsal
Read over the instructions in this exercise and memorize the procedures and the spoken words. As discussed above, rehearse the elements of this spell until you can perform each step seamlessly.

Stage 3. Self-Preparation
For a few minutes, invoke the *Law of Pretending. Pretend* that you are skilled and experienced at casting spells. You have been practicing magic for many years. You are about to cast this practice spell in an attempt to re-experience what it was like when you first started to practice magic.

Stage 4. Physical Preparations
A raised working surface or *stand* and this book is needed (page 75). You will also need a half teaspoon of ground mace and a half teaspoon of dried rosemary to make an incense. Both herbs are available in the spice section of most supermarkets. Mix the two ingredients together and wrap this incense in a piece of folded

parchment or put it in a small covered container made of any material but plastic. Keep this for later use during the ritual. An incense holder and an incense charcoal are also necessary. These two items are available in occult shops, religious supply stores and sometimes in import stores that carry a selection of brass items from India. Instructions for mixing and burning incense and for making your own incense burner can be found in appendix 5. A lighted white or yellow candle is needed as a means of lighting the incense charcoal.

Prepare the rosemary cleansing tea ahead of time as described on page 78. Purify all of the various materials you will be using in the ritual, including the incense, incense holder and charcoal, candle, cleansing tea, its chalice or vessel, your working surface, clothes, etc. Purify *Foundations of Magic* and any bridge jewelry as bridge symbols (see page 74). As these are *bridge* symbols you will **not** need to purify this bridge jewelry or the book again for future spells.

Place all of the items to be used in this ritual on the *stand* in the center of the area in which you plan to cast your circle. Change into your ceremonial clothes and remove your everyday jewelry just before performing your ritual. Open *Foundations of Magic* to a Practice Spell (Appendix 4, page 235). Light the candle.

Stage 5. Ritual

- Center yourself (page 76).

- Cast and cleanse your magic circle (pages 76–79).

- Proclaim your *intention* by saying the following words from memory:

  "This ritual is well and truly commenced to accomplish the purpose of my Will which I proclaim to be as follows . . ."

  "To experience magical space and to learn about the magic within this circle that I have cast, and to claim its sanctuary as mine."

- Ascend to your *higher state* (page 59).

- Light the incense charcoal with the candle flame and place a small pinch of the mace and rosemary incense on top of it. The smoky vapors of both herbs stimulate psychic and mental awareness. Be aware of their essence as you begin.

- See the interior of the circle. Can you see the boundary of the space the circle defines? What does it look like? What do the objects and surfaces within the circle look like? What do you see with your eyes and what do you see with your imagination? As you spend more time in this magical space, these two ways of seeing will begin to merge, but only while in the circle.

- Feel the interior of the circle. What does it feel like to be in the circle? Do you sense the protection and the sanctity offered by the circle? What does the air feel like? How does your body feel? How is your mind?

- Listen inside the circle. Notice the quality that silence has in the circle. Say something out loud and notice the sound of your own voice. Gently splash the cleansing tea with your fingers and notice the quality of sound it makes.

- Attend to things outside the circle. As viewed from inside your circle, how do things outside the circle look different from those inside of it?

- What is the quality of that difference? What do you notice about the sounds that emanate from outside the circle? Remind yourself that all everyday concerns lie outside the circle. Briefly think of one. Notice how its power to affect you is absent or greatly diminished.

- Direct your *Will*. Forcefully speak the following proclamation out loud. As you speak, be aware of your *Will* being directed out beyond the boundaries of the circle, out to every corner of the universe to effect your purpose. Also be aware of your *Will* simultaneously being directed inward to every corner of yourself, for you are the microcosm that corresponds to the macrocosm, which is the universe.

  > **"Let my awareness, appreciation, and effective use of magical space increase boldly and rapidly and for the good of all. I Will it so with harm to come to none."**

- Descend from your *higher state* (page 60).
- Disperse the circle (page 80).

Stage 6. Follow-up
A few hours after you have dispersed your circle, reflect on the experience of having performed this ritual. For most people the shift in perception that occurs inside

the magic circle is immediate. For others there is no apparent difference, at least in the beginning. This disparity in initial response is not an indicator of the levels of later proficiency. Everyone's awareness increases with practice and each person comes to each new realization about magical space in their own time. Know that you are doing well.

When a Spell Doesn't Seem to Work

One of the biggest surprises for people who are new to the craft of magic is how frequently and effectively spells work. A conscientiously cast spell usually gets the job done. Occasionally, however, you will work a spell and nothing seems to change. When this occurs it's time to do some troubleshooting. It is best to approach this with enthusiasm and a sense of opportunity. The best time to learn new skills is when something doesn't work. Remember that if you are not encountering failures, you are not learning since you are obviously only doing what you already know how to do. It can be, therefore, a bonus when you cast a spell that doesn't work. Examining what may have gone wrong can put you in touch with things about yourself or aspects of your life that had hitherto lay hidden.

Lack of Recognition

The first thing to determine is whether or not something actually has changed and you are not yet aware of it. Often the very outcome we seek comes in such a different form than we imagine that it is hard to recognize. There is an old and often repeated parable that illustrates this quite nicely. Although most people have heard this story in one of its many versions, it is worth repeating.

A merchant who became separated from his camel caravan finds himself alone and on foot in the desert. He wanders lost for several days and soon runs out of water, gradually becoming weak and sick from overexposure to the Sun. Lost, thirsty, and ill, he begins to pray for God's help. God hears his prayers and, seeing his predicament, decides to talk to him directly. "You have always been a good and pious man and are deserving of my help. I will soon deliver you from your plight." Overjoyed that God heard his prayers, he sets off with renewed vigor. Soon, after cresting a large sand dune, he meets another camel caravan. The leader of the caravan welcomes him to join them and says that they are passing right through his village. The merchant thanks the caravan leader, but declines the offer, explaining that God's help will be coming at any time now. The caravan moves on, leaving him alone again in the desert. Soon he comes across a lone trader who has with him several camels laden with water bags. The trader, imagining that the merchant must be very thirsty, offers him as much water as he can drink. The merchant is grateful but explains that the trader should keep his water, as God will soon take care of him. A few hours after the trader has disappeared over the horizon, the merchant comes upon an old wandering tribeswoman who sees his sun blisters and realizes how sick he is. She explains that she is the healer of her tribe and she can help him. Once again he declines assistance, explaining that God's help is imminent. On the following day dehydration and sunstroke overcome him and he dies. His immortal soul drifts up to the gates of heaven where God greets him. Confused, the merchant says, "O Holy of all holies, why have I died? You spoke to me yourself and promised to deliver me from the desert." With considerable chagrin God replies, "Seldom have I met such an ungrateful mortal. I sent you a trader to quench your thirst, a healer to cure your sun sickness, and a caravan to take you home, and you refused each one. Of course you died, you fool."

Be alert to the possibility that a successful spell may manifest in ways you had not anticipated. If you are fortunate, you may some day encounter one of the most exquisite occurrences in spellwork. It is the special case where you have always had what you've wanted and the spell changes nothing but your recognition of that fact.

Poorly Formed Intention

Sometimes, despite your best efforts, you will work a spell to a purpose that is simply not right for you or someone else. Take, for example, the criterion that harm shall come to none. It may be that realizing your *intention* will bring harm in ways that you don't recognize. Alternatively, your *intention* may violate some aspect of free *Will,* or run counter to the *true nature* of yourself or someone else.

What may be out of alignment with your *intention* is timing. The time that your conscious mind wants an event to occur or a change to materialize can be all wrong based upon other overriding, broader considerations. This is a good place to keep in mind the old nostrum that the universe is unfolding as it should. Magic works within the framework of the unfolding universe, not counter to it. The most practical approach, if you suspect timing is a factor, is to rework the spell at a later date and see what transpires then.

There are any number of other ways in which your *intention* could be flawed. For example, it may be impossible or highly improbable. In the event of an unrealized *intention* it is a good policy to review your *intention* in the context of the design guidelines discussed at the beginning of this chapter.

Poor Execution

As with any other task, from time to time you can make an error or mistake when casting a spell. Perhaps you inadvertently leave out a section of the *Ritual,* or speak some of the words incorrectly, or miss something in the preparation phase. Depending on the nature of the error or omission, mistakes can render a spell less effective or even completely ineffective. Attention to detail and increased familiarity when preparing and practicing magic will usually minimize these problems.

Of more concern is intentional deviation from procedures of a spell. Unfortunately, it is common for people to assume that they can abbreviate or otherwise modify the design of a spell. This is particularly common with the preparation stages that some may be tempted to either ignore altogether or perform in a cursory or half-hearted manner. Imagine being an inexperienced cook attempting to follow a recipe for making bread. What would happen if you decided that the yeast, which is called for in such a small quantity, could just as well be left out, or that letting the dough rise just to be punched back down again was an unnecessary step? This is completely analogous to making changes in a spell when you don't fully understand the role of each part. When you gain experience and skill as a cook, you can begin to vary recipes in ways that make sense and produce the desired results. With enough experience you can even begin to create your own recipes. The same holds true for magical spells. Until you become a practiced magician, follow the procedures in *Foundations of Magic* exactly as described.

No Reason

Human beings are addicted to reasons and explanations. Usually, if we examine a situation enough, we can emerge with reasons why something happened or didn't happen, or happened in the particular way that it did. Seldom are our explanations tested, and often they have little to do with any inherent truth. All we require to be satisfied is that our reasons and explanations adhere to a malleable kind of internal consistency that supports our existing beliefs. One of the most uncomfortable notions to the human mind is the possibility that some things happen for absolutely no reason. Comfortable or not, sometimes it is necessary to recognize that there is no reason why a particular spell didn't work.

Ethics

Integrity

There is one overarching law when working magical spells, whether for yourself or for others. It is the basis for maintaining integrity in your work with magic and deserves to be writ large and remembered first and last:

DO NO HARM.

If you follow this simple edict and are honest with yourself, you will remain free of the tangled intrigues and dangers that inevitably accompany black magic.[8] To support this principle, most of the spells in *Foundations of Magic* include a spoken declaration that harm shall come to none, and the spells are designed so that they become ineffective if this directive is ignored.

Working Spells for Others

Working a spell in order to help someone else requires more care, and is fraught with more potential pitfalls than working a spell to help yourself. In general, the practice is best undertaken after a person has gained a thorough grounding in spellcraft through experience. For this reason only one spell in *Foundations of Magic*, Helping Another Person Achieve a Willed Purpose (page 201), is suitable for working for the exclusive benefit of another person. (Helping Your Distressed Plant or Animal, on page 211, can, of course, be worked for a plant or animal friend.) Be sure you have ample familiarity working spells for yourself before you attempt to use this spell to help someone else.

---

8. As *Foundations of Magic* is entirely a work of white magic, little is written here regarding the dangers of black magic. One example that may warrant a brief mention, if only for the sake of illustration of such dangers, is the magical principle of "three times rebound." The intended effects of a curse against someone who has a strong personality or is psychically well protected can bound back to curse the person casting the spell, but amplified three times.

It is easy to be wrong about someone else's needs simply because we rarely know all the relevant information about their circumstances or experience. In order to compensate for the effects of this lack of information there are number of guidelines that must be followed when working a spell for others. Heed the following advice:

1. Whenever practical, get the other person's permission.

2. Whenever practical, work with the other person to form the *intention* of the spell and only work with an *intention* that both you and the other person agree upon 100 percent.

3. Form an *intention* which, above all other considerations, works in harmony with the other person's free *Will* and *true nature*.

There are times when it may be legitimate to work a spell for another person without them knowing about it. For example, there may be someone who you genuinely believe would benefit from a specific spell worked on their behalf, but they do not believe in magic or may otherwise be uncomfortable with it. Before you proceed, examine your motives for helping them and be very careful about what *intentions* you choose for them. Be very sure you have given number 3 above its full due. Be willing to receive no recognition or credit from anyone for the help your work may provide, and keep silent as discussed in chapter 1.

In the absence of complete, accurate information about someone or their situation, it is often better to work with the essence of an *intention* (see page 69) rather than attempting to be precise about it in detail. For example, in working a spell to assist Jim, our single parent, you could cast a spell for him to "take the next necessary step in his life to increase his fulfillment as a parent and to improve the quality of life for both him and his child."

About the Format in Part II

Part II contains the instructions for casting each spell in *Foundations of Magic*. Many of the procedures in the preparation stages are essentially the same for all spells and therefore are not repeated in the instructions. For example, *Designing a Well-Formed Intention* and *Rehearsal* are not included in the spell instructions because it is understood that both these stages must be completed in a similar manner for all spells. Likewise, the instructions to center yourself before beginning a ritual are omitted from the *Ritual* instructions as centering is a part of every spell. Nor are preparing the normal rosemary cleansing tea, purifying the materials, or changing into ceremonial clothes mentioned in the *Physical Preparations* instructions.

For a better understanding of how the instructions for each spell are presented, turn to appendix 4 where you will find the instructions for Exercise 8, A Practice Spell (page 81) formatted in the same manner as all of the other spells in Part II.

Be Prudent

Before moving on to Part II of this book, an elaboration on the *Law of Prudence* (page 25) is in order. Once the power and effectiveness of casting magical spells is experienced, it can be tempting to start relying on them exclusively as the only means to achieving goals. Don't give in to this temptation or, paradoxically, the magic you work will become diminished and ineffectual. Magic requires that you be committed to your *intentions*. Lack of normal, prudent action on your part demonstrates a lack of sincerity and commitment. If you are seriously ill, work the spell Transforming Chronic or Serious Illness (page 126) **and** see a doctor or other health professional. If you need a job, work Achieving a Willed Purpose (page 198) **and** diligently search the "help wanted" ads. If you have lost your car keys, work Finding a Lost Item (page 164), **but first** look for them. It is foolish, and in some cases dangerous, to neglect the obvious means to accomplish something. Magic can work where all other means fail. Nevertheless, magic must be worked in conjunction with prudent action, as it does not work well for fools or the insincere.

Part II

THE SPELLS

ATTRACTING SOMEONE
FOR FUN AND LUST

This simple ritual mobilizes raw Will power and amplifies it with the beauty and power that are part of physical and aesthetic attraction. The centerpiece of the ritual is a magical sonnet.

Be aware that you are working in an arena where there is great potential for both you and other people getting hurt. If harm is a sure consequence of consummating the attraction, then the spell will not be effective and the object of your desire will remain free of your influences. Circumstances change, however, and if things don't work out now, cast your spell again at a later date.

Self-Preparation

Create the clearest image you can of the person you wish to attract. Next, as an observer, see a clear image of yourself. With magic there is no need to exaggerate this image in any way. Form an image of yourself that is as accurate as possible. Then, again as an observer, see the two of you together. Remain as emotionally detached as possible as you view your mental image. Your emotions will be needed as a source of energy during the ritual.

Physical Preparations

Place a chair and a stand in the center of the location where you plan to cast your circle. Have the chair facing east.

Ritual

Cast and cleanse your circle, and face east.

Proclaim your intention and be seated in the chair.

Ascend to your higher state.

Visualize the two of you together. Upon arriving at your higher state, again perform the exercise outlined above in Self-Preparation. To repeat, create the clearest image you can of the person you wish to attract. Next, as an observer, see a clear image of yourself. With magic, there is no need to exaggerate this image in any way. As before, form an image of yourself that is as accurate as possible. Then, again as an observer, see the two of you together. Remain as emotionally detached as possible as you view your mental image.

Switch from observer to participant. Very briefly, as a participant, experience what it would be like to be with this person in the way you have visualized. Only do this long enough for your full feelings of desire to come to the fore. When this occurs, hold on to these feelings and read the following magical sonnet with the full force of these emotions.

> With immodest pleasure I gaze upon thee.
> A dam that stops the carnal river's flow,
> Your form and countenance does build in me;
> And desire's reservoir fills to overflow,
> While moist thoughts of you add dangerously,
> To mounting pressure from this swelling lake;
> I muse about you most libidinously,
> Hoping and waiting for this dam to break.
> But now enough wishing for fate to serve,
> For I Will you to draw down Eros' pool;
> And I shall use magic without reserve,
> As my Will is always my ultimate tool.
> > I Will thee come to me now; make it so,
> > And to no one come any manner of woe.

Descend from your higher state.

Disperse your circle. LET GO and allow the magic to work.

Follow-up

After casting this spell, unexpected and perhaps unusual ideas about accomplishing your purpose may occur to you seemingly out of nowhere. Act on them.

ATTRACTING THE
RIGHT LOVE PARTNER

This spell is to be used when you are interested in a specific person as a potential love partner, and it is intended to accomplish two things. First, it is designed to help you determine if the person you are attracted to is right for you in a long-term committed relationship. Second, if the person is right for you, this spell works to increase their attraction to you. If you have no specific person in mind but are looking for a love partner, then Finding Love on page 102 is the spell you need to work.

Self-Preparation

Center yourself. Reflect on your attraction to this person, and on your desire to have a partner. Forget all the advice you may have received on this subject, and forget your own self-talk on the subject. This is a time to have a completely receptive mind, free of the many preconceptions that usually accompany this endeavor. When you feel your mind is clear and you are open to new information (or old information from a new perspective), then ponder the following questions:

- Why do you want a partner?

- What is it about this person that attracts you?

- How well do you know this person?

- How does this person treat other people?

- What are the key personality characteristics of the other person?

- If you were to be characterized, what are the key characteristics of your personality?

- How well do the key characteristics of both of you match?

- What qualities would you bring to this relationship?

- Are you being dishonest with yourself in any way about this relationship?

- Are there any questions about the other person or yourself that you are afraid to ask?

It is alright if you do not get clear answers to some of these questions. Any ambiguities or uncertainties will be addressed, at least at the unconscious level, while working the spell. Because honest answers will come from working this spell, prepare yourself for the possibility that you may receive an answer you will not like. Remember that it is best to receive any negative news at this preliminary stage of a relationship rather than later on, when the stakes are much higher. Also, remember that the answers you receive only apply for now. Things can change and, although not common, working this same spell at some later date may occasionally result in different answers, even if you have the same person in mind.

During a pivotal part of the ritual, you will mentally project an image of a Y indicating "yes" or an N indicating "no." This projection must happen quickly and unconsciously. Prepare yourself for this procedure by answering the following "yes or no" questions by projection. Stare at a blank wall. Instead of answering the question in words, or even word thoughts, visualize a large Y or N, whichever is appropriate, superimposed on the wall. Let the visualized image come quickly without conscious thought on your part. Practice this until it seems natural.

- Are you a male?

- Are you a female?

- Do you live in North America?

- Do you live in South America?

- Do you have a dog?

- Do you have a cat?

- Are you over 40 years old?

- Are you under 40 years old?

- Do you have green skin?

- Do you have two eyes?

To become practiced at this, you may need a longer list of "yes or no" questions. Be sure to write any additional questions down before you attempt to answer them by projection. All questions should be trivial questions to which you definitely know the answer. If you have persistent difficulty with this task, then invoke the Law of Pretending and pretend you see either a Y or an N.

Physical Preparations

Yarrow is a powerful love charm and in this spell it is used both as a preparatory bath and as a cleansing agent in the ritual. Prepare 2 cups of yarrow tea by pouring boiling water over about a teaspoon of dried yarrow leaves or 2 teaspoons of fresh yarrow. Steep the mixture until it reaches room temperature and then strain it, discarding the yarrow leaves and stems. Place the strained tea in the refrigerator until you are ready to use it.

Shortly before casting this spell take a brief seven-minute yarrow bath. Pour 1 cup of the yarrow tea into the bath water, but do not use soap or other toiletries. Sit peacefully in the bath, with no other intention than to let the magic of the yarrow work. Three times during the bath, submerge yourself completely, head and all. At the end of seven minutes, allow yourself to air dry in a warm room, then dress for casting your spell.

You will need to prepare three talismans for this ritual.[1] As this spell exposes your love interest to the full light of truth, all three will be solar talismans using the Magic Square of the Sun. Follow the instructions in Appendix 6. On the first talisman, trace the sigil of your love interest and write the number 1 on the opposite side. On the second talisman, draw the sigil of your name and write the number 2 on the opposite side. On the third talisman, draw both of your sigils, one superimposed on the other, and write the number 3 on the opposite side.

Place the three talismans in a line, in numerical order with the number sides up, on the stand in the center of the area where you will be casting your circle.

---

1. Talismans are objects that are individually tailored to concentrate energy, Will, and magical influences. They are used to help the person casting the spell direct these forces to a purpose. The type of talisman used here is but one of countless varieties used in many magical traditions.

Ritual

Cast and cleanse your circle, and face east. Use the remaining yarrow tea to cleanse your circle in the same manner that you would normally use rosemary tea.

Proclaim your intention.

Ascend to your higher state. Read the following words as if you are making a pronouncement both to yourself and to the universe, speaking with firmness and conviction:

> Enamored am I of this one;
> Desirous am I to be close,
> But before any pursuit is begun,
> My condition I must diagnose.
>
> Three answers to three queries,
> Will provide the knowing I require,
> And 'tis the following magical series,
> 'Twill bring the rejoinders I desire.

Look down at the first talisman and read the following words. As you read, be aware of the question that is being posed, and trust that the truest and best answer will come when later you turn the talismans over.

> Is this one best and right for me?
> I Will that this be answered swift and true,
> For my heart may not let me see,
> That his [her] nature I misconstrue.

Look down at the second talisman and read the following words. As you read, be aware of the question that is being posed, and trust that the truest and best answer will come when later you turn the talismans over.

> Am I right and best for this one?
> I Will that this be answered swift and true,

For even if my heart be won,
In time, my love he [she] may eschew.

Look down at the third talisman and read the following words. As you read, be aware of the question that is being posed, and trust that the truest and best answer will come when later you turn the talismans over.

Is it best for all that we two intertwine?
I Will that this be answered swift and true,
For even if for the other we each shine,
Our whole is more than the sum of us two.

One by one, turn each talisman over. The instant you turn one over, see either a Y or an N projected on the sigil side of the talisman. Do this for each one in turn.

If there are Ns among the three projections, then read the following words. Again, read as if you are making a pronouncement both to yourself and to the universe. Speak with firm conviction.

The answer be "nay" to one [two or three] of these,
With caution let the magic start,
To look for a way that by degrees,
My true nature can make peace with my heart.

In the future I may enact this ritual again;
Seasons pass and new eclipses old;
A more opportune time for this campaign,
May arrive when "yes" appears threefold.

OR

If there are three Ys, then read the following words. As you read, project the full force of your Will with every word. Let the universe hear you. Give strength to your magic.

The answer is "aye" to all three;
Attraction magic, at once commence;
Pull him [her] to me I decree;
Draw him [her] with boldness and diligence.

Magic, be as forceful as any force ever seen;
Pull all stops bar none; clear away every impediment;
Move us together with no obstacles between,
And harm come to none as no harm is meant.

Descend from your higher state.

Disperse your circle.

Follow-up

If you had three "yes" answers, then fix your attention on your love interest, set your mind to the purpose, and then LET GO and allow the magic to work.

If you had a "no" answer, then focus your attention on resolving the conflict between your present desires, your true nature, and higher knowing. Perhaps this is the catalyst you need to make some desired changes in your life. It may be that the time is not right for this union; at some future date, you may cast this spell again, with different results. Above all, be grateful for the truth.

FINDING LOVE

This spell is intended for those who are looking for a lover, but have no one specific in mind. If you are trying to attract someone you already know (or know of), then either Attracting Someone for Fun and Lust on page 93 or Attracting the Right Love Partner on page 96 would be more appropriate.

Self-Preparation

Center yourself, and reflect on your search for a lover and, perhaps, a partner. Forget all the advice you may have received on this subject, and forget your own self-talk on the subject. This is a time to have a completely receptive mind, free of the many pre-conceptions that usually accompany this endeavor. When you feel your mind is clear and you are open to new information (or old information from a new perspective) then ponder the following questions:

- What are you looking for in another person?

- Why do you want a lover?

- Do you have unrealistic expectations or standards?

- Do you have too few standards?

- What characteristics are you willing to be flexible about?

- What do you need to do to increase your chances of meeting the right person?

- In what places or within what group of people do you presently look?

- What do you do that prevents you from meeting the right person?

- What can you do that is entirely different from anything you have ever done before?

- How would you recognize this person if you met them?

Pay careful attention to your own answers to these questions, and pay particular attention to the questions for which you have no answers.

Physical Preparations

Prepare a cup of yarrow tea by steeping about a teaspoon of dried yarrow leaves or 2 teaspoons of fresh yarrow in a teapot. Yarrow is a very common plant and can be gathered in many areas during the good weather months. It is also readily available in herb shops and some health food stores.

A chalice (separate from the one used for rosemary cleansing tea) or a small, round-bottom bowl is required. It is important that the bottom of the inside of the bowl or chalice not be flat—not even a flat spot. You will also need two glass orbs (marbles). One of the orbs will represent your future love and should be completely clear glass (no coloring). The other orb will correspond to you and should be chosen with care. Be sure that it suits you. Place the teapot, chalice or bowl, and the orbs on a stand in the center of your working area.

Ritual

Cast and cleanse your circle, and face east.

Proclaim your intention.

Ascend to your higher state. Read the following words as if you are making an announcement to the universe:

> Rare and untarnished is the love I have for thee;
> Love so pure, love most clear, love without regret.
> A perfect love is ours but for small formality;
> We know each other not, for we have never met.

Pick up the orb corresponding to you and drop it into the chalice or bowl. As you do, read the following words:

> This small orb corresponds to me,
> And the vessel to the love we'll share.

I await in love's center for thee,
To drop in from out of thin air.

Pick up the clear orb corresponding to your future love, then drop it into the chalice or bowl and recite:

This small orb corresponds to thee,
And the vessel to the love we'll share.
The sure pull of desirous gravity,
Forms the singularity that is a pair.

Pour the yarrow tea slowly into the chalice or bowl until it covers about two-thirds of both orbs. Fix your gaze on the orbs and recite the following over and over again with increasing volume and tempo, feeling the tension build. Speak the words as if you are broadcasting a message to the universe. Continue until you feel your magical message has been sent to every corner of the universe.

Come my love
With dispatch
Hand in glove
Perfect match
Mind & spirit
Body & heart
Perfect fit
From the start
Best for me
I Will it done
Best for thee
Harm to none

Sit for a few moments in silence, after you have stopped reciting.

Descend from your higher state.

Disperse your circle.

Follow-up

Place the chalice or bowl (with the tea and orbs still in it) in a safe place, where others will not discover it. Leave it there until the yarrow tea evaporates. LET GO and let the magic work.

SPELL FOR AN UNFAITHFUL LOVER

Like the ritual for Attracting Someone for Fun and Lust (page 93), this spell mobilizes raw Will power and its centerpiece is a magical sonnet. This is essentially a form of binding spell, where all of the wayward lover's efforts to cheat are turned back upon themselves, resulting in an ever increasing preoccupation with you. This is not a spell that works by violating free Will, however, and its effectiveness only works in the arena of cheating or unfaithfulness. If your lover has left you and openly taken up with someone else in accordance with their free Will and true nature, then the spell will have no effect.

Self-Preparation

You must prepare by finding within yourself the rage that this situation breeds. Then you must go past the act and feeling of rage in order to gain access to the power and energy fueling that rage. Rage is very powerful, but it is not focused; it can bring you as much grief as benefit. It is the pure personal energy at the source of the rage that can be directed and put to magical use.

For some people, having an unfaithful lover hurts so much that they cannot even find the rage underneath their pain. If you are in this situation, your first step is to get mad; do whatever you have to do to get angry. If you have persistent difficulty getting past your pain to anger, then invoke the Law of Pretending—pretend you are angry as hell. One of the best aids to successfully pretending to be angry is to forcefully vocalize your anger and make angry gestures. Pound on a pillow, chop firewood, rant to an understanding friend, or yell.

It is important that you don't misunderstand the intention here. Anger will not solve your problem, but it will put you in touch with an enormous reservoir of energy and personal strength. Once in touch with it, the trick is not to waste this extremely liberating force by dissipating it on further expressions of anger. Each time you really get in touch with your anger, pause and bring your attention to the energy behind it. This is pure untransformed energy. It is not aggressive, revengeful, mean, or violent, nor does it possess any other emotional quality; but it is immensely forceful and powerful. This is what you have at your disposal to work the purpose of your Will in this spell.

Physical Preparations
Place a stand in the center of the area where you will cast your circle.

Ritual
Cast and cleanse your circle, and face east.

Proclaim your intention.

Ascend to your higher state.

Find the energy at the source of your anger, as you did in the Self-Preparation phase. This will usually happen quite quickly in your higher state. Do this by getting in touch with your anger, and then quickly move past it to its source.

Become completely infused with your own pure energy. This is energy you will utilize, not as anger, but as personal strength and the unstoppable force of Will, for this purpose. Visualize the energy permeating and surrounding you, and when your strength is that of a lion and your voice can be that of the lion's roar, read the sonnet. Be sure you have familiarized yourself thoroughly with its meaning and meter.

> My heart does not suffer such a fool,
> As one whom would my precious love spurn;
> And no pain of lost trust will make me mewl,
> For this roaring that bids, "Intrigant, learn!"
> So with Lion's voice and Lion's breath,
> I Will magical mischief be freed from its lair;
> And when you plan your next little death,
> My hunting pride will thee tightly ensnare.
> Eyes opened or closed all you will see,
> Is my abiding image encircling you;
> And all thoughts and feelings will be of me,

With no escaping for love's prey so untrue.
  Cease thy infidelity; I Will thee, abstain!
  And none be afflicted with any more pain.

Show yourself as you wish to be seen. Slowly turn clockwise, making several rotations on your own axis, and display to the universe who you are. As you turn, hold your arms up and out, not in the manner of a supplicant, but rather as someone fearlessly demonstrating power and presence.

Project your image to your unfaithful lover. Face the direction you believe your wayward lover to be located, and form an image of them. Prepare to project your present image directly to your wayward lover. Start by reciting the words below, slowly and softly. Continue to repeat them again and again, increasing the volume and tempo as you do. Feel the tension of your psychic energy build. When you intuitively feel the energy has reached a maximum level, boldly speak the words one more time, releasing the built-up energy as you do. Visualize the energy carrying your projected image directly into your lover's consciousness.

> *See thou well*
> *I stand before thee*
> *See thou well*
> *With thine Will that's free*
> *See thou well*
> *I Will thou see me*

Stand in silence for a few minutes. Know you have sent a very powerful and influential message. Know that if it is right for your lover to abandon infidelity and return, it is now certain that they will do so, for strong magic is at work. Remind yourself that your lover has free Will and must live in accordance with their own true nature, and this cannot be violated. Remind yourself of your own power and strength when you live and act in accordance with your own true nature.

Descend from your higher state.

Disperse your circle.

Follow-up

If you find yourself in emotional pain in the days that follow, get in touch with your anger. When you are angry, go past your anger and find the energy behind it. Remember, this energy is a remarkable resource for experiencing your own strength free of pain or vindictiveness. Go through your days under the influence of this energy. Speak of none of this with your lover.

HELP IN PARENTING

(Providing Your Children with Guidance)

Communications between adults and children are imperfect at the best of times. Each child and each parent has their own different disposition and interests. Children grow up in a different time and often in a different social setting than their parents did. Children need to assert their individuality (and eventually their independence) at the very same time that their parents are attempting to set certain behavioral standards and establish some degree of control. Parents have a natural instinct to protect their children, and yet children are constantly exposed to such risks as sickness, accident, drugs, alcohol, cigarettes, and violence. Parents have absolutely no choice as to which part of their own behavior their children will unconsciously choose to model. No two parents seem to ever completely agree on how their children should be raised, and no two children respond in the same way to whatever parenting methods are used. As anyone who is a parent knows, this list of parenting challenges could go on for pages. Any clear-thinking person, who takes the time to assess the difficulties inherent in being an effective parent, could easily come to the conclusion that it can't be done.

This spell is intended to assist in guiding the parent casting the spell as well as the child or children for whom it is cast. It takes into account the enormous range and variability of parenting opinions and options. It also recognizes that, regardless of how frustrating it is at times, children are individuals, have free Will, and make many of their own choices. The magic in this spell addresses the difficulty of determining what is best for our children by acknowledging the universal aspirations of all parents.

If you have more than one child whom you wish to benefit from this magic, cast a separate spell for each child, preferably on different days.

Self-Preparation

Special care is required when forming your intention for this spell. It is natural that parents want the best for their children. Care is required in determining what "the best" is and how to get it. The effectiveness of this spell and your success at guiding your children depend on working with, and not against, a child's true nature. In gen-

110

eral, it is best to keep your intentions free of absolutes and predetermined solutions (such as going to college or taking music lessons or becoming a doctor). If, however, you are committed to a certain course of action or specific solution, then temper your conviction with a genuine resolution to respect each child's true nature as preeminent. This allows you to be wrong and still accomplish your goal of wanting the best for your children.

Act as if you have a clear mind, a strong and open heart, steadfast love, patience, perseverance, and forgiveness for your mistakes and theirs. If you believe you cannot find all of these things within yourself, pretend you can. Form your intention from this place.

Physical Preparations

Sage is associated with acquiring wisdom and maintaining a clear mind. It is used both as a preparatory bath and as a cleansing agent in this ritual. Prepare 2 cups of sage tea by pouring boiling water over several sage leaves or 2 teaspoons of dried sage. Steep the mixture until it reaches room temperature, then strain out the sage. Place the strained tea in the refrigerator until you are ready to use it.

Shortly before casting this spell, take a brief seven-minute sage bath. Pour 1 cup of the sage tea into the bath water, but do not use soap or other toiletries. Sit peacefully in the bath, with no other intention than to let the magic of the sage work. Three times during the bath submerge yourself completely. At the end of seven minutes, allow yourself to air dry in a warm room, then dress for casting your spell.

Ritual

Cast and cleanse your circle, and face east. Use the remaining sage tea to cleanse your circle in the same manner that you would normally use rosemary tea.

Proclaim your intention.

Ascend to your higher state.

Visualize your child as they would be when in a completely receptive state. Then read the following words with compassion and conviction, as if you were reading them directly to your child:

By the magic I weave
I'll ensure you possess
Gifts that relieve
Much of life's stress
Gifts which, I believe,
Never cause distress
Nor true nature aggrieve
Nor free Will oppress

Chant and continue to visualize your child. Start with a firm voice, but with a low volume and slow tempo. As you continue to visualize your child, repeat the chant over and over again. Increase both the volume and tempo as you repeat the words. Feel the energy build:

Safety's caress
Love, to receive
Love, to express
Success to achieve
Health to possess
Seldom to grieve
Act from goodness
And joy inweave
May wisdom bless
And folly take leave

Discharge the psychic energy when you have built it to the point of climax, usually about 30 seconds after the build-up starts to become uncomfortable. When you reach this point, repeat the chant one more time. Then, at the very point of discharge, speak the following words with maximum force and volume, feeling the force of your Will bursting out on the tremendous stream of your psychic energy.

I Will it so!

Sit in silence for a few minutes, knowing you have sent strong magic into the world in a pure act of Will. Take advantage of the quiet and clarity of your mind, and notice if any ideas, impulses, or insights related to your parenting come to consciousness. Speak the following words:

No harm to thee
No harm to me
So mote it be

Be receptive to any clarity that comes your way. LET GO and let the magic work.

Descend from your higher state.

Disperse your circle.

HEALING AN INJURY

This spell works by entering magical time and appealing to the universal truths, which are revealed in the correspondence between the microcosm (your body) and the macrocosm (the universe). For your body to be injured, the universe must be injured. This apparent absurdity leads to the magical conclusion that your injury is a lie. It is not a lie that you are injured, but rather your injury itself is a lie, a universal lie. Swift healing comes from studying the truth and revealing the lie by exposing it to the light of time past and time future.

Self-Preparation

Enter into a light to medium trance. Remember a time shortly before your injury occurred, a time when you were completely free of the injury. Fully experience the following in your mind:

First, as a participant, remember what it felt like to be free of the injury. Narrow your attention to the affected area on your body and, as fully as possible, get in touch with the normal feeling of having that body part in perfect working condition. Feel yourself using that area of your body. Feel what it is like to touch, or bump or squeeze this area and have it be pain-free. If this is a place on your body that you can easily see, what does it look like in its normal healthy state?

Next, view this part of your body free of injury, but this time as an observer. As an observer, you can see yourself from any vantage point, so look at this area from several perspectives. These observations should, of course, be made as if there are no clothes or other impediments to your full view.

Make all of your images as clear, colorful, and focused as possible. If there is a particular spot that is painful or damaged, zoom in on it—see what it looks like before the injury. Zoom back out—see this spot normal and healthy in the context of your whole body. With moving pictures, watch your healthy body work and move easily and normally. Be thorough in your observations.

When you have completely familiarized yourself with what your body looked and felt like just prior to the injury, imagine a time in the near future when your injury is completely healed. Repeat the same process, both as participant and as observer, for this future memory. Feel and see yourself and the relevant parts of your body free of injury, healthy and working normally. Be thorough.

If you have been injured in more than one place, then repeat this entire procedure, recalling past and future memories for each part. When you feel that you know your normal, healthy, functioning body in both the past and the future, end your trance.

Physical Preparations

Place a stand on the Southern edge of the area where you plan to cast your circle. When the circle is cast, the center must be free of objects. Place matches, and a yellow candle in a holder, on the center of the stand.

Ritual

Cast and cleanse your circle, and face east.

Proclaim your intention.

Light the candle.

Enter a light to medium trance, and face west. Read the following words, speaking firmly and projecting well, as if you are reading a proclamation to the universe:

The memory mirrors do reflect,
Where past and future intersect;
Into the mirror of yore I'll gaze,
As my unclad body it displays;
An image of some yesterday me,
Hale and free of injury;
One place on me I scrutinize,
This, where my present impairment lies.

Visualize a large magical mirror materialize in front of you. This is a mirror of the past and reflects only past events. Allow an image of your unclad body, from a time in the past, shortly before your injury occurred, to form in the mirror. As you practiced in the preparation phase, view your body at a time when you were completely free of the injury. View the image in the mirror as an observer, not a participant. Be thorough. See the relevant part of your body from different angles and see it moving or working in its true healthy state. Now, speak the following words from memory. Repeat them, out loud and with firm conviction, for each new image or each new perspective you view on your healthy body.

I see it healthy
I see it whole
I study it well
With all my soul

Face east and read the following words. As before, speak firmly and project well—as if you are reading a proclamation to the universe.

The memory mirrors do reflect,
Where past and future intersect;
Into the mirror of morrow I'll gaze,
As my unclad body it displays,
An image of some future me,
Hale and free of injury;
One place on me I scrutinize,
This, where my present impairment lies.

Visualize another large magical mirror materialize in front of you. This second mirror reflects only future events. Allow a near-future image of your unclad body to form in the mirror, your injury completely healed. Once again, be thorough and see the relevant place on your body from different angles. See it moving or working in its true healthy state. Now, speak the following words from memory. Repeat them, out loud and with firm conviction, for each new image or each new perspective you view on your healthy body:

I see it healthy
I see it whole
I study it well
With all my soul

Stand in the center of the circle, facing south. Visualize the mirror of the past still materialized on your left (east) and the mirror of the future still materialized on your right (west). As before, read the following proclamation:

> **The memory mirrors do reflect,**
> **Where past and future intersect;**
> **Both mirrors truly reflect me,**
> **And swift healing of my injury.**

Gaze into the candle flame. Without looking either to the right or left, feel that you are reflected in both mirrors. As long as your intuition indicates, allow your body to learn the truth.

Come back up out of trance.

Disperse your circle. LET GO and allow the magic to work.

ALLEVIATING CHRONIC PAIN

Pain is intended to protect us by alerting or warning us of illness or injury that needs our attention and care. Long-term chronic pain, however, is almost always the result of a well-intentioned mistake. The mistake occurs when pain lingers long past its usefulness, when warnings and protection are no longer needed. It is as if the "fasten seat belt" signal in your automobile were to stay on after you have fastened your seat belt. In both cases, the seat belt signal and pain's signal only serve as an extreme irritant. Most people who suffer from chronic pain derive no further benefit from pain's signals.

Nevertheless, the particular pain you feel may still be serving you in a useful, protective, or warning capacity at specific times, or under particular circumstances. Remember that when pain is not mistaken, it is valuable feedback. To ensure that pain can return to you for a short period, if it is needed, a witness object is incorporated into this spell. The object works on old magical principles of association and correspondence and should be kept on your person or nearby after casting the spell.

The design of this spell recognizes that the mistake of chronic pain must be demonstrated—while at the same time, the beneficial aspects of pain must be appreciated and respected—if it is to dissipate and fade into the background.

Self-Preparation

Spend a few moments and, both as a participant and then as an observer, remember what it was like for you to be free of pain. As a participant, feel yourself in various situations where you are free of pain, and notice how normal that feels. Then, as an observer, see yourself in these same situations. Take a good look at yourself free of pain. If your pain has been with you a very long time and you cannot remember a time when you were free of it, then picture someone else who is similar to you in many ways but is free of your pain. First, as an observer, see them. Next, feel what it is like to be them. As a participant, experience yourself as this other person in various situations, where you are free of pain, and notice how normal that feels.

Ready your imagination for the experience of being in two places at once. Imagine for the moment that you are sitting on a warm beach. Now, imagine that you drift back out of your body, so that you can see yourself sitting on the beach. There are

118

now two "yous"—the "you" who is sitting on the beach, and the "you" looking at the "you" sitting on the beach. Have the first "you" (the one sitting on the beach) drift over to where the second "you" is observing, and merge with the second "you." Now there is just one "you." Practice shifting between these different perspectives and different "yous."

Physical Preparations

Place a stand in the center of the location where you plan to cast your circle. If your condition prevents you from standing, place a chair next to the stand. Have the chair facing east. A witness object is needed. A horse chestnut is legendary for its magical powers of pain relief, and is therefore ideal. If one is not available, any palm-sized charm, such as a stone, crystal, or special coin, can be used. The charm should be purified and placed on the stand before the circle is cast.

Ritual

Cast and cleanse your circle, and face east.

Proclaim your intention.

Ascend to your higher state.

Hold the horse chestnut or charm in your left hand. Continue to hold it throughout the ritual, until it is time to disperse your circle. Take a moment of quiet reflection and consider something that is usually overlooked by someone who has suffered from chronic pain. Pain, when it is not a mistake, is a protective ally. There is a universal wisdom to pain and, even when it manifests as a mistake, pain deserves our respect and appreciation because the intention behind it is one of service to us. From your higher state, feel the appreciation that this intention to serve merits, and find the goodwill to approach pain as a friend. Read the following words while standing, facing east. Direct your Will to correct the mistake of chronic pain, expressing yourself from a place of understanding and appreciation.

> **The Guardian of Paradise, my Pain;**
> **The voice of un-articulated alarm;**

Unflinching, relentless, ever watchful,
The harsh friend protecting me from harm.

Your standards are most high;
You trust in none but you;
But as your grateful charge I ask,
You recognize the changes due.

The flowing tide prepares to ebb;
The thunder has begun to cease;
The call is for subtler ways,
As time turns round with sure caprice.

Your work is done, your wisdom learned;
Take leave old warrior and find respite;
Retire loyal friend, it is rest you need;
Still your voice most erudite.

Others will stand guard for you;
Mind and spirit, blood and bone;
Love and friendship will heal and mend,
With no need for you to chaperone.

Rest dear pain;
Be peaceful dear friend;
Your work for now,
Is at an end.

Visualize your astral body leaving your physical body and traveling in the astral plane. From your position inside the circle, see your astral body travel outside of the circle and into a region of the astral plane where the mistake of unnecessary pain is automatically recognized and corrected.

See yourself with the mistake corrected. From within the sanctity of your circle, view your astral body as it is, free of pain. Look carefully as your body moves through everyday activities easily and with no discomfort. It is common for some people to have their consciousness flip back and forth between their astral body and physical body. It is alright if this happens. Continue viewing your body as it is, at ease and free of pain, until you sense that the mistake has been completely corrected.

Direct your astral body to rejoin your physical body. When you are finished viewing, visualize your astral body traveling back to your circle and rejoining your physical body. As the joining occurs, many people experience a very strong sensation of body changes. Others notice no difference and are not consciously aware of pain relief until after they disperse and leave their circle. Just LET GO: let the magic work and move on to next part of the spell. Now, recite the following words from memory. As you do, focus your gaze on the horse chestnut or charm while you hold it out in front of you.

> *Stand witness small charm,*
> *As pain has bid adieu;*
> *And warn of pending harm,*
> *With signals clear and true;*
> *This covenant to alarm,*
> *Is binding hitherto.*

Descend from your higher state.

Disperse your circle.

Follow-up

Carry the horse chestnut charm with you. You have established a magical contract with it. It will protect you from harming yourself while you are free of pain. You will receive a strong signal, either a feeling or an image, which will warn you if you are doing anything to further injure yourself.

ALLEVIATING ACUTE PAIN

This spell is designed to give relief from relatively short-term pain that originates from a specific injury or affliction. Longer-term chronic pain is better addressed by casting the spell Alleviating Chronic Pain on page 118.

This spell makes use of one of the many extraordinary transformations that are possible in magical space. Pain, the body sensation, is transformed into pain, the visual experience. This metamorphosis provides great relief from physical discomfort.

It is important, however, that you retain the beneficial character of pain, that is, its protective and warning function. Remember, pain is a signal that some part of you needs attention or protection. The witness object in this spell provides you with a way for your body to signal you if you are doing something that threatens to further aggravate your injury or affliction.

Self-Preparation

All of our experiences have at least three components—a seeing component, a feeling component, and a hearing component (some experiences also have taste and smell components, but they are not relevant here). Even if we are not consciously aware of it, our mind translates everything that happens to us, including the experience of pain, into some sort of picture, feeling, and sound. It just so happens that, in our everyday conscious mind, the feeling component of pain is so loud that we cannot usually notice the other two. You could say that when it comes to pain, our conscious mind usually has a prejudice in favor of feeling. There is, however, no such prejudice in magical space.

You will need a clothespin in order to proceed with the practice exercise. Clip the clothespin to one of your fingers, or to a fold of loose skin on your arm. Position it so that you can plainly feel the pressure, but it is not painful. Enter into a medium to deep trance. Having achieved the desired trance state, gaze at the location where the clothespin is clipped and be aware of the feeling of pressure. As you continue to gaze, imagine that the pressure has a color, and allow your mind to visualize a muted hue of this color slowly starting to appear around the area where the clothespin is attached.

Take your time. Slowly increase the depth and brightness of the color. As the color of the pressure becomes brighter and deeper, know that the pressure feeling is decreasing at the same rate. The brightness of the color will reach full intensity when there is no more feeling of pressure.

When a complete transformation from feeling to vision occurs, allow the intense color to assume its own amorphous form, and have it start to drift slowly away from your finger or arm. Visualize it drifting to a free-floating position a few feet out in front of you.

Once you have the amorphous form of the pressure's color in front of you, watch it as it spreads out over your entire visual field. Notice that it spreads itself thinner and thinner, so that the color becomes more and more faded and faint. Finally, see it as it spreads out far and wide, so that it becomes completely undetectable in extreme dilution.

Take a minute to be aware that the original pressure has transformed to a color that has become so dissipated that it is undetectable. Bring yourself up out of trance and remove the clothespin.

Practice this exercise several times. It is best if you can become proficient at this task before casting your spell, but it is not necessary. If for any reason you experience difficulty, pretend that you can do it with ease. When you are casting your spell, the power of Will, when used within the magical space of the circle, will greatly amplify the results of this process.

Physical Preparations

Place a chair and a stand in the center of the location where you plan to cast your circle. Have the chair facing east. A witness object is needed for future use as a symbol and a signal. A horse chestnut is legendary for its magical powers of pain relief, and is therefore ideal. If one is not available, any palm-sized charm (such as a stone, crystal, or special coin) can be used. The charm should be purified and placed on the stand before the circle is cast.

Ritual

Cast and cleanse your circle, and face east.

Proclaim your intention.

Read the following words. Speak firmly and project well. You are directing this straight to your own pain, but you want the universe to hear it clearly. Read with conviction, as if every word originated from within you.

> Pain,
> No need to leave me;
> I bid thee grow stronger instead,
> But change thee from a feeling,
> To a vision of crimson red.
>
> As pure scarlet pain,
> Bring no sensation, just hue;
> To increase thy domain,
> Move out beyond my skin,
> Where I can watch thy fine show,
> And not sense thee within.
> Shine big and bright in the atmosphere,
> Stay until thou tire and fade,
> Then grow faint . . . and still . . . and disappear.

Enter a medium trance. Before entering trance, be seated in the chair. Once you have attained a satisfactory trance state, hold the horse chestnut or charm in the hand that is on the opposite side of your body from the source of pain. Shift your focus to the source of the pain. Look directly at the spot. If the spot is on your back, or in some other surface location which you can't see directly, visualize it by staring at it in your imagination. If it is an internal pain, imagine looking right into your body—to the very source of the pain.

Transform the feeling to a vision, as you did in the Self-Preparation exercise. The procedure is repeated here. Remind yourself now that you can change the feeling of this pain to a vision of pain. As you continue your gaze, know that the pain has a red color and visualize a muted hue of red slowly starting to appear around the affected area. Take your time. Slowly increase the depth and brightness of the color. At the same rate that the color of pain becomes a brighter and deeper red, know that the pain is decreasing. The brightness of red will reach full intensity when there is no more feeling of pain.

Direct the red color outside of your body. Allow the intense red to assume its own amorphous form, and have it start to drift slowly away from the afflicted area. Visualize it drifting to a free-floating position a few feet out in front of you.

Direct the vision to disperse. Once you have the amorphous form of pain's color in front of you, have it start to spread out over your entire visual field. Have it spread itself thinner and thinner, so that the color becomes more and more faded and faint. Have it finally spread out far and wide, so that it becomes completely undetectable in extreme dilution.

Come back up out of trance and ascend to a higher state.

Hold the chestnut or charm out in front of you, focusing your vision on it. Recite the following words from memory:

> *Stand witness small charm,*
> *While pain remains a view,*
> *And warn of pending harm,*
> *With signals clear and true;*
> *This covenant to alarm,*
> *Is binding hitherto.*

Descend from your higher state.

Disperse your circle.

Follow-up

Carry the charm with you for the length of time you need its help. You have established a magical contract with it. It has been witness to the transformation of physical pain to imaginary pain, and it will protect you from harming yourself while you are free of pain. You will receive a strong signal—either a feeling or an image—that will warn you if you are doing anything to exacerbate your injury or affliction.

TRANSFORMING CHRONIC OR SERIOUS ILLNESS

(Being Witness to the Creative Side of Magic)

At first, the concept behind this ritual may seem to be an odd one, even for magic. Because of this, the procedure for this spell can be difficult to comprehend for those who first encounter a description of it. Once the concept is understood, however, the steps are easy to follow. In casting this spell, you will be engaging in a conversation with the source of your illness. As usual, your conscious part of the conversation will be conducted mostly with words. The source of your illness, however, will converse with you by means of visual and feeling metaphors, and occasionally with word-thoughts.

You will be working strong magic on yourself and you will be using the most creative aspects of magic to do so. When you have completed your ritual, you will have some insight into this most remarkable notion: much of the same creative magic that goes into producing an artistic masterpiece goes into producing an illness and into curing an illness.

Self-Preparation

With your hands, gently massage the area of your body most closely associated with your illness (i.e., the area that is most painful or uncomfortable, most vulnerable, or nearest the organ most involved). Slowly explore with your massaging until you can find the point of greatest response. If the area that you need to massage is awkward to reach, then it is best to recruit another person to massage you. This should be someone you are completely comfortable with, as you will be including them within your circle when you cast your spell.

The next step involves a little mind game. Imagine there is a benign magical entity with which you would like to communicate. If it helps you get started, you can give the entity a name and imagine it in a specific location. For instance, it may be called Mantic, who lives at the center of the Earth, or Philimon who dwells in another dimension. Allow your imagination free reign. The entity talks mostly in images and feelings, and when it does use words, it speaks only in word-thoughts. You, of course, converse mainly in words. Enter a light trance, then speak out loud to this entity and say, "What do you think about the state of the world?" (Or pick some other subject, but, for the purposes of this preparation exercise, do not choose your illness). Be attentive and notice what images come to mind, what feelings or words pop into your head. These will be the communication from the entity. Continue to let your imagination take its course. In most cases, the predominant response will be a mental image. If no image spontaneously comes to mind, make one up. If the image, feeling, or word-thoughts don't completely answer your question (and at first they rarely do), either ask another question, or make a comment in an attempt to elicit more information. Here are a few examples of questions or comments that may help you:

- I see an image of [whatever image is in your mind]. To what part of the image should I pay the most attention?

- Show me more.

- I get a certain feeling. Can you send me a picture (or word-thoughts) that elaborate on the feeling?

- None of this is clear to me, even at the intuitive level. Please give me the same information in a different way that I can understand intuitively.

- Does this picture have anything to do with [name what it is you believe the image or feeling means]?

The last question is a "yes or no" question. You may receive an answer back as a simple word-thought, or you may have to establish a signal system with the imaginary entity. For instance, you could ask the entity to increase a certain feeling, or the brightness of a mental image, for "yes," and decrease it for "no." Then, when you ask a "yes or no" question, the increase or decrease will give you an answer. You are encouraged to play with this imaginary conversation. Continue as you would in any conversation where you are attempting to understand another person. Do not concern yourself with completing this process or establishing a meaningful conclusion. It may seem like a rather peculiar amusement, but it will help prepare you for a real conversation with the real source of your illness.

Physical Preparations

You will need whatever is required to allow you to be comfortable while you massage yourself (or someone else massages you). You could use a mat and pillows on the floor, a massage table, or a chair (and perhaps one for the other person if there are to be two of you). The furniture should be arranged so that the part of you that is being massaged is located in the exact center of where you plan to cast your circle.

Ritual

The following instructions are written as if you will be casting this spell by yourself. If you have someone who will be assisting you with the massage, then make the obvious adjustments in procedure. Remember that, at any point in the following ritual, you may invoke the Law of Pretending.

Cast and cleanse your circle, and face east.

Proclaim your intention.

Enter a light to medium trance.

Gently massage the area associated with your illness (i.e., the area of your body that is most painful or uncomfortable, most vulnerable, or nearest the organ most involved). As in the Self-Preparation phase, slowly explore with your massaging until you find the point of greatest response. Continue to gently massage this area throughout the remainder of this ritual. When you have found the appropriate spot, quiet your mind, so that it is open and receptive for whatever comes. Read the following words out loud, projecting well past your circle for the entire universe to hear:

> The highest of high magic I summon to me;
> The magic of creative transcendence,
> Which will tease out the mythical imagery,
> From within the depths of my dissonance.
>
> I Will that high magic does presently,
> Deliver a visual offering,

Which wells from the source of my malady,
And hence from the source of its curing.

Allow any image to emerge from your mind. This image, although originating from the source of your illness, will likely not have any obvious connection with your illness and, in most cases, it is better if it doesn't. An image may form almost immediately, or you may have to wait a while. Also be aware of any feelings or word-thoughts that may emerge. Your images, feelings, and thoughts are the raw material for this magic's art, similar to the way in which clay is the material of the sculptor or metaphor is the material of the writer.

Find within yourself a sense of gratitude and appreciation for these simple mind materials, and for the sacredness of the place of wisdom within you from whence they dawned. Find this gratitude even if the image is just empty blackness, or if there are disturbing aspects to the image. Read the following words as an expression of that gratitude:

It is with the deepest respect and gratitude,
That I encounter the source of this metaphor;
And it is with a sense of beatitude,
That I become its magical interlocutor.

Start a conversation with your own psychic metaphor. This metaphor comes directly from the seat of your illness. Your intention in doing this is to have the metaphor shift and change and reveal. In engaging in this communication, your conscious mind is communicating directly with other aspects of yourself through the medium of creative magic. This is you learning important knowledge about yourself, but not in the usual rational or intellectual manner of your waking thoughts. It is important that, as you continue your communication, you avoid the trap of needing to understand the nature of what you are learning in any explicable way. Although occasional or even frequent insights will often occur during this ritual, they are, at least in these beginning stages, more peripheral than central to your healing. Continue with your communication, watch your metaphor develop, and let the magic work.

Be aware of what is shifting in you. Remember to continue your gentle massage. During this entire process be aware of what is stirring and transforming in you. At some point, your metaphor will begin to make intuitive and emotional sense. As this starts to occur, there is generally a lessening of your symptoms and the beginning of feelings of well being, increased hope, or an overall lessening of the experience of being ill. Eventually, you will sense that this process is coming to completion. At this stage, it is quite common for people to experience either a complete absence of their symptoms or a dramatic decrease. If this does not occur at this time, it often follows within a few hours or days of the ritual. When you intuitively know the magic communication of the ritual is complete, read the following words:

> I honor and praise my own magical skill,
> For the healing that's here been done;
> That it continues to work I proclaim is my Will,
> With no harm to me or to any one.

Come back up out of trance.

Disperse your circle. LET GO and let the magic work.

ELIMINATING AN ALLERGY

An allergy is a particular kind of mistake that your body makes in an attempt to protect you. It is similar in this way to the mistake of chronic pain (Alleviating Chronic Pain, page 118). When the allergen (the harmless substance to which you are allergic) enters your body, your immune system mistakenly perceives it as a threat and mobilizes to defend against it. Our suffering comes from the mistake, not the substance. This spell utilizes your imagination to allow you to astral travel to a place where this mistake can be corrected.

Self-Preparation

If your allergy is triggered by a specific, known allergen, then take the time to think of something that is similar to this allergen, but that is benign and produces no allergic reaction in you. For example, perhaps you are allergic to wheat flour, but not to oat or rice flour. If you are allergic to bee stings, perhaps you are not allergic to wasp stings. You may be allergic to goldenrod pollen, but not mustard flower pollen. The benign substance should be as similar to the allergen as possible.

If you have an allergic reaction but you are not aware of the specific allergen, then think of a situation where you would have this reaction, and then think of a very similar situation in which you would not. For example, in the spring you may be allergic to some unknown plant material in the air, and when you breathe your allergy is triggered. Think of a situation in the spring when you can breathe, without the reaction (such as at a beach, in the shower, or in an air-conditioned building).

Remember what it is like to be exposed to the substance or situation that causes the allergic reaction. Go into the memory as a participant, and re-experience what it is like to eat (or breath, or touch, etc.) this allergen and suffer from the allergic response. Pay attention to your skin, lungs, eyes, or whatever parts of you are normally affected. Notice how each part feels, and in what way it causes you discomfort.

Next, remember what it's like to be exposed to the substance or situation that does not cause the allergic reaction. Again, go into the memory as a participant and re-experience what it is like to eat (or breathe, or touch, etc.) this substance, in this situation without any immune system responses. Pay attention to your skin, your lungs, your eyes, or whatever parts of you are normally affected. Be aware of what these parts feel like free of discomfort.

Now, as an observer, view yourself. See yourself exposed to the substance or situation that does not trigger an allergic reaction. Pay attention to all of the same things you noticed as a participant; but this time, view yourself as if you were watching a movie of yourself.

Ready your imagination for the experience of being in two places at once. Imagine for the moment that you are sitting on a warm beach. Now imagine that you drift back out of your body so that you can see yourself sitting on the beach. Now there are two "yous"—the "you" sitting on the beach, and the "you" looking at the "you" sitting on the beach. Have the first "you"—the one sitting on the beach—drift over to where the second you is observing, and merge with the second "you." Now there is just one "you." Practice shifting between these different perspectives and different "yous."

Physical Preparations
Place a chair and a stand in the center of the location where you plan to cast your circle. Have the chair facing east.

Ritual
Cast and cleanse your circle, and face east.

Proclaim your intention. Then be seated in the chair.

Enter a medium trance.

Visualize your astral body leaving your physical body and traveling in the astral plane. From your position inside the circle, see your astral body travel outside of the circle and into a region of the astral plane where the mistake of perceiving the allergen as a threat is automatically recognized and corrected.

See your astral body experiencing a normal response. From within the sanctity of your circle, view your astral body being exposed to the substance or situation that is similar to the allergen, but that does not cause the allergic reaction. Remember, you are in your circle observing your astral body outside of the circle. Similar to what you did in the Self-Preparation procedures, see your astral projection eating (or breathing, or touching, etc.) this substance and being free of any immune system responses. Pay attention to your skin, lungs, eyes, or whatever parts of you are normally affected. Be aware of what these parts look like when you are free of the allergic discomfort. This is a view of how your body responds to substances about which it has never made a mistake.

See your astral body correct the mistake. Now, direct your astral body to repeat what you have just observed. This time you're exposed to the old allergen, but the allergic mistake has been corrected. See your astral projection eating (or breathing, or touching, etc.) what used to be the allergen, and watch your body respond in the same appropriate manner as it just did with exposure to the similar substance. See your astral projection eating (or breathing, or touching, etc.) this substance and being free of any immune system responses as it always should have been. The mistake is corrected.

Direct your astral body to rejoin your physical body. Visualize your astral body traveling back to your circle and rejoining your physical body. As the rejoining occurs, many people experience a very strong sensation of bodily changes. Others notice no difference and are not consciously aware of anything until the next time they encounter the old allergen and find their old reaction is gone. Just LET GO: move on to the completion of the spell and let the magic work. Read the following words out loud. Increase both the tempo and volume of your voice as you read, culminating in a loud forceful climax as you read the last line "no harm to anyone."

> O harmless creation of God we need never war again;
> I soon will enter your world and you shall enter me;
> The errors of the past, no longer do they pertain,
> For you have a new identity, no more the enemy.
>
> With you I now swear a solemn truce;
> I know now what matter you be,
> And your true nature I can educe,
> From the false phantoms I used to see.

And NOW my Will be done;
No harm to me, no harm to you,
No harm to anyone.

Come back up out of trance.

Disperse your circle.

ATTRACTING MONEY, SHORT-TERM

This spell is used to attract a specific amount of money. For increasing your regular flow of money, work Attracting Money, Long-Term on page 138.

Self-Preparation

Take a few minutes to reflect on any actions you can take (aside from working this spell) to increase your chances of receiving the money you need. Actively working toward your goal in every practical way will increase this magic's effectiveness.

Physical Preparations

Place a blank piece of parchment (or good quality paper), a pencil, and an eraser on a stand located in the center of the area where you will cast your circle.

Ritual

Cast and cleanse your circle, and face east.

Proclaim your intention.

Ascend to your higher state.

Write the word "MONEY" very neatly in capital letters across the center of the parchment. As you do this, say the following words:

> *On this parchment with care I apply*
> *The erasable letters M-O-N-E-Y.*

Erase the M and the Y from what you have just written so that only the letters O, N, and E remain. As you do this, say the following words:

The M & Y I take away
Then the word for 1 is on display.

Erase the O and the E, so that only the letter N remains. As you do this, say the following words:

Next I remove the O & E
The letter "N" is all I see.

Erase the N, so that no letters remain. As you do this, say the following words:

I erase the N without a trace
And all that's left is a band of space.

Again, declare your intention by reading the following, speaking so that it is heard and understood by all the magical forces in every corner of the universe:

I stare into this space and start to count,
And stop when I arrive at the correct amount.
The amount must always reflect true need;
The spell is broken if I succumb to greed.
Now I take my pen in hand,
And write the amount in the empty band.
I write the amount in numerals bold,
And then thrice the paper I do fold,
And when this paper is hidden away,
Then money to me, BE ON YOUR WAY!

Start counting from zero. You will be counting dollars (or pounds sterling). You can count by ones, fives, tens, hundreds, or—in extreme cases—thousands. Use whichever counting system seems most fitting.

Write down the amount. Once you have counted up to the amount you want, stop counting and write down the number on the parchment in the same location where the word MONEY was previously written.

Fold the paper three times. Fold it first across its width. Turn it 90 degrees and fold it again. Turn it once more and make the last fold.

Descend from your higher state.

Disperse your circle.

Follow-up

Place the folded paper in a safe place. Proceed with any activities you believe will help bring in the money. LET GO and allow the magic to work.

ATTRACTING MONEY, LONG-TERM

In this spell, you will use the influence of incense, a very old magical charm design, and the power of Will to achieve your purpose. It is intended to increase your regular income. If you are looking for a one-time injection of funds, work the spell Attracting Money, Short-Term on page 135.

As both the preparation phase and the ritual have many different parts to consider, be sure to familiarize yourself thoroughly with the procedures and obtain all the necessary materials. Every aspect is important.

Self-Preparation

Center yourself, and reflect on your past and present actions aimed at bringing in money. Reflect on your beliefs, and on your thoughts and feelings about money, by asking yourself the following questions:

- How much money do I need?

- How much more than that do I want?

- How much feels like too much (greed)?

Take some time to picture yourself as having all the money you feel you need and want. Then, picture yourself having more money than you feel you need and notice at what point it starts to feel like greed.

- What do I do or fail to do that gets in my way of having the money I want?

- What do I do that helps me draw the money I want?

Take this time to get to know your relationship with money intimately.

Physical Preparations

To prepare the money-attracting charm required for this spell you will need a small cloth pouch, a whole nutmeg, a drop or two of mercury (quicksilver), an eyedropper, a red candle or red sealing wax, and a small amount of pure extra virgin olive oil. The pouch can be made of any natural fabric other than silk and should be just large enough to contain the nutmeg.

A few words of caution regarding mercury are in order. Due to health and environmental concerns in recent years, stringent laws and regulations regarding mercury procurement, storage, use, and disposal have been enacted in many jurisdictions. It is a toxic substance and should be handled with care, avoiding direct skin contact. Under no circumstances should it be ingested. Mercury obtained for the ritual should be stored or disposed of in an approved manner. This precaution also pertains to items that have come into contact with the mercury, such as its container and the eyedropper. There are a variety of sources for mercury. An old mercury thermometer, a mercury switch out of a defunct electronic component (such as an old low voltage wall heating thermostat), or a child's chemistry set are three possible sources that you may have around the house. If you don't have any of these items, check with local junk stores. Sometimes you can acquire the small amount required from a laboratory or scientific supply house. If procuring and handling mercury proves too daunting, you can use dill or fenugreek seeds instead, since both of these plants correspond to mercury and to matters of attracting money. Nevertheless, if you can manage it safely, mercury is preferable.

To make the charm, drill a small hole (approximately ⅛-inch diameter) about half way through the nutmeg. Using an eyedropper, place a drop or two of mercury in the hole, or place one or two dill or fenugreek seeds in the hole. Once the mercury or its corresponding seeds are inside, seal the hole with red wax.

To make a money-attracting incense, you will need a teaspoon of dried basil, a teaspoon of dried pine needles, and a teaspoon of benzoin gum. Benzoin gum is available in, or can be ordered from, most health food stores or herb shops. Mix the three ingredients together and wrap the mixture in a piece of parchment, or put it in a small covered container made of any material but plastic. This will be used as incense during the ritual. For the purposes of this ritual, it is best to have a swinging type incense holder, sometimes referred to as a "censor," and an incense charcoal. These are available in occult shops, religious supply stores, and sometimes in import stores that carry a large selection of brass items from India. Instructions for mixing and burning incense and for making your own incense burner can be found in Appendix 5.

In readiness for the ritual, place the stand in the center of your working area. On it, put the mixed incense, the incense burner, a lighted yellow candle, the sealed nutmeg charm, the pouch, and a small container of olive oil.

For this ritual, your working area is your entire house or apartment (you will be casting your circle around the entire premises). For this reason, you should work this spell when no one else is present. The stand should be located in a central place in your home.

Ritual

Cast and cleanse your circle, and face east. As already mentioned, cast your circle large enough to include your entire home. As you will be immediately using incense, there is no need to practice your usual cleansing ritual with the rosemary tea. The incense is designed to both cleanse and set the stage for attracting money.

Proclaim your intention.

Light the incense charcoal with the candle flame and, once lit, place several large pinches of the incense on top of it. As you are lighting the charcoal, speak the following words from memory:

As I light this consecrated incense
Let the ritual of money commence
And prepare my home for Prosperity
For prosperous I intend to be

Incense your entire house. With the incense burner in your right hand and the container of incense in your left hand, silently circulate through your house to every room, including the basement or cellar and the attic, if it is a walk-up attic. While gently swinging the incense holder, bring the incense into every corner of every room, thoroughly censing the entire house. As you are doing this, keep your focus firmly on your intention. Notice anything that may occur to you regarding your ability to earn more money. If the incense burns out while you are circulating through the house, add some more to the charcoal. When you are through, return to the stand. Set the incense or burner on the stand and let it burn out in this location.

Ascend to your higher state and face east.

Anoint the nutmeg by rubbing olive oil on it, and as you do, be aware that you are creating an entity that is "alive" in a magical sense, and whose sole purpose is to assist you in attracting the increased income you desire. As you rub on the oil, read these words:

> With this oil thou art anointed,
> To ancient magic serve.
> As my charm thou art appointed,
> To gain the bounty I deserve.

Place the oiled nutmeg in the pouch and hold the pouch firmly in one hand. Pick up this book in the other hand, and read the following words:

> Now it is me who must prepare,
> And make ready to act my part true.
> In my actions I must be ever aware,
> To hold to my true nature whatever I do.
>
> I Will that I am guided by the magic I effect,
> Along the path of my own right-livelihood.
> In the sanctity of this circle I will introspect,
> Upon what is needed for my monetary good

Stand silently within the quiet sanctity of your circle. Take a few minutes to reflect on your relationship with money and your actions to acquire it, just as you did in the Self-Preparation exercise. You are now in your higher state, and you have put strong magic to work. Notice any thoughts, feelings, images, or insights that may drift even briefly into your consciousness. Be aware of your charm and its ability to magically assist you, and remind yourself that strong magic will only work if you are active and play your right and true part in improving your financial situation.

Descend from your higher state.

Disperse your circle.

Follow-up

For the next three weeks, keep your amulet with you, but out of sight, throughout the day. You can put it in a pocket or purse, or wear the pouch under your shirt or blouse on a string around your neck. At night, keep it near you, but safe and out of sight.

Once a week for the next three weeks, cast and cleanse a circle in the place where you usually practice magic and ascend to your higher state. Start the ritual by once again holding your charm in both hands and repeating the part of the spell beginning "Now it is me who . . ." Once again, quietly explore your relationship with money by reflecting on the same considerations as those of the previous week. Notice if any things have changed from the proceeding week(s). Notice if you have any new ideas or inspirations. Which aspects of your relationship with money feel solid and which feel shaky? When you feel complete with this process, close your circle and put your charm back in its normal location. During the periods between rituals, LET GO and allow the magic to work.

Improving Your Business or Career

This spell is designed to bring you increased success in your career or business, and thereby increased prosperity. At its basis is the understanding that you must fully do your part, consistent with your true nature, to bring about the desired improvements. As these improvements are realized, magic will work to ensure that the rest of the world does its part.

Self-Preparation

Set aside at least a couple of hours (and perhaps more) to complete this phase. You have many things to consider. In the instructions and questions that follow, substitute the word "career" for the word "business" if it is more appropriate to your situation, and disregard any questions that do not apply.

Reflect on yourself and on your actions aimed at improving your business. Reflect on your beliefs, thoughts, and feelings about business in general, and your work in particular.

- Does the work itself fulfill you?

- How much of what you do each day is dissatisfying or odious?

- How much of your workday do you enjoy?

- Of the work you fail to enjoy, how much of the dissatisfaction could you eliminate by changing your opinion of, or attitude toward, the work?

- How much of what you do runs contrary to your true nature and how much is in alignment with your true nature?

- How are your actions and responses to your business affecting your close relationships?

- How are they affecting your health?

- Where are the problem areas that have been limiting the success of your business?

- How much of this is within your power to change?

- If you cannot affect all of the necessary changes yourself, who can help?

- What questions do you not ask yourself because you don't even think to ask them?

- What are the strengths of your business and what are the weaknesses?

- What could be simplified?

- What improved?

- What added?

- What eliminated?

- Do you believe in what you and your business are doing?

- If you don't, are there changes that you could make to put it right?

- Have you ever considered leaving your business for some other pursuit?

- Who are you working with?

- How have things changed?

- If you take some time to picture yourself as having the success in business that you have always wanted, how does it look?

- In this scenario of success, what are you doing?

Do a "consideration inventory" of your business. Start with the material objects used in your business (for example, staplers, chairs, tools, light fixtures) and consider each one in relation to you and to the part it plays in your business. Be aware of what occurs in thoughts or feelings as you consider each of these things. No part of your business is too small to consider, even down to such things as where you keep your paper clips. Do a consideration inventory on the following:

- Small objects (e.g., stapler, pliers, paper clips)

- Electronic or electric equipment or tools

- Large equipment (e.g., tractor, printing press)

- Furniture, art, and decor (e.g., wall hangings, plants)

- Facility (e.g., house, building, factory)

- Lighting

- Vehicles

- Fellow workers or employees

- Customers or clients

- Consultants

- Your product or service

- Your competitors' product or service

- Your books

- Your bank

Get reacquainted with the intimate details of your business, and see how they relate to you and your goals for improvement.

Physical Preparations

Soak 7 shelled almonds and 7 thin slices of fresh ginger together in 2 cups of water for twenty-four hours. Remove the almonds and ginger (soaked almonds are delicious and quite suitable for eating) and keep the liquid for use during the ritual, as a sprinkle and cleansing water, in place of the usual rosemary tea.

To make incense, you will need a teaspoon of ground cinnamon and a teaspoon of benzoin gum. Benzoin gum is available in, or can be ordered from, most health food stores or herb shops. Combine the two ingredients and wrap the mixture in a piece of parchment, or place it in a small covered container made of any material but plastic. Keep this for use as incense during the ritual. An incense holder and an incense charcoal are also necessary. These are available in occult shops, religious supply stores, and sometimes in import stores that carry a large selection of brass items from India. Instructions for mixing and burning incense and for making your own incense burner can be found in Appendix 5.

Place the chalice or cleansing vessel, incense holder, charcoal, incense, and a lighted yellow candle on a stand in the center of the area where you plan to cast your circle.

Ritual

Cast and cleanse your circle, and face east. Use the almond and ginger water to cleanse your circle rather than the usual rosemary tea.

Proclaim your intention.

Ascend to your higher state.

Visualize your main place of business while facing in the direction where it is located. See the image as clearly as you can, as if you were actually standing looking at it. Sprinkle (flick almond and ginger water with your fingers) this projected image seven times. Once you have done this, let the image fade.

Light the incense charcoal with the yellow candle and place two pinches of the incense on it. Be quietly aware that you will be under the influence of the essence of its smokey vapors for the remainder of this short ritual. Read the following words with firm conviction:

> As I light this consecrated incense,
> Let this ritual of improvement commence,
> And prepare my business for Prosperity,
> For prosperous I intend it to be.
>
> Now it is me who must prepare,
> And make ready to act my part true.
> In my business activities [career] I must be aware,
> To stay true to my nature whatever I do.
>
> I Will that I am guided by the magic I effect,
> To bring right-livelihood into full realization.
> In the sanctity of this circle I will introspect,
> Upon what I need do for a prosperous vocation.

Stay in silence within the quiet sanctity of your circle until the incense burns out. Be aware that you are in your higher state. Reflect upon the things that occurred to you during your Self-Preparation work. Think about your business, and allow any thoughts or feelings to come freely to the surface. Be aware of any new thoughts or insights that may occur to you now.

Descend from your higher state.

Disperse your circle.

Follow-up
Pour the remaining almond and ginger water into a container with a lid and take it to your main place of business. Remove the lid, and place the open container somewhere where it will not be disturbed. Leave the container there until all of the liquid has completely evaporated. Repeat this entire ritual once a week for the next three weeks, except do not use the almond and ginger sprinkle. Instead, cleanse your circle as you normally would with rosemary tea. During the last part of the spell where you reflect on your business considerations, notice if any things have changed from the preceding week(s). Notice if you have any new ideas or inspirations. Act on them.

LUCK AT GAMBLING

The old fashioned power of magical plants is employed in this spell. This can be very effective for the occasional gambler's short runs of good luck. If you are a compulsive gambler, this spell will bring you no results, as any compulsion inhibits your ability to realize your true nature. And do not become greedy, as greed mobilizes its own kind of black magic.

Self-Preparation

Take a few minutes to pretend the following. Imagine that you are holding a piece of High John the Conqueror root (or any of the other good-luck botanicals that are listed below), and that the root is an agent for the forces of chance and luck. Imagine that the root and you can communicate on some very deep level beyond words or thoughts, and that the root is learning about you. At the same time, you are receiving from it the very essence of what constitutes good luck. Do this in silence, and let your own intuition determine when you are complete.

Physical Preparations

Choose one, and only one, from the following list.

- 3 whole pieces of High John the Conqueror root (see footnote 2, following page)
- 3 Lucky Hand roots (see footnote 2, following page)
- 7 hazelnuts
- 11 holly berries if you are male, or 7 ivy leaves if you are female
- 11 strawberry leaves
- 7 rosehips and 7 rose leaves

For convenience, the word "roots" is used in the instructions that follow. This should be understood as referring to whatever plant material (berries, leaves, nuts) you have chosen from the list above.

148

Place the roots in a small glass, wooden, or pottery bowl (avoid plastic or metal), and put the bowl on a stand in the center of your working area.

Ritual

Cast and cleanse your circle, and face east.

Proclaim your intention.

Ascend to your higher state.

Hold the bowl of roots, cupped in both hands out in front of you, at about heart level. While looking at the roots, recite the following words from memory:

> *Ancient agent of magic,*
> *Herb of good fortune,*
> *In this circle omophalagic,[3]*
> *With you I shall commune.*

Visualize the energy of the roots and your energy mixing and mingling in the space around the circle. Imagine a communication between you and the roots, but not one of words, rather one of essences and energies. At a deep unconscious level, learn what the roots have to teach about achieving good luck. When this feels complete, say the words:

> *I Will that this be done,*
> *And harm shall come to none.*

---

2. High John the Conqueror (which is poisonous) and Lucky Hand (also known as Hand Root or Salap) may be more difficult to locate than the other plants, unless, of course, you happen to live where they grow. Their uncommonness may work to your advantage if you go out of your way to procure either of them, as this spell is sometimes rendered more effective if significant effort is expended.

3. Omphalos denotes a legendary stone at Delphi in ancient Greece, considered to be the center of the earth.

Descend from your higher state.

Disperse your circle.

Follow-up

Place the bowl of roots in a dark, dry place, such as a closet or cupboard, where it will not be disturbed. When you need good luck—for example, when you buy a lottery ticket or bet on a horse—carry a piece of the root next to your wallet or money holder. When its immediate work is through, return the root to the bowl. Whenever your luck runs well, place some coins in the bowl with the roots for gratitude, and leave them there.

This ritual can be repeated every six months to a year in order to recharge the good luck magic. When you are through using the magic of the roots, give the coins to someone who needs them more than you.

REALIZING SELF-ESTEEM
(Or Recognizing the Immutable Aspect of One's True Nature)

At the core of this spell is a recognition of one of the most profound human truths: one's self is completely separate from one's behavior, appearance, beliefs, strengths, weaknesses, or any other personal characteristic. Your self is unchangeable and immeasurable, and therefore cannot be improved upon or impoverished in any way. This is an elusive concept for some, and even for many who understand it intellectually, it may be difficult to experience. The very strong magic in this ritual will give you the ability to know this truth directly. Once you do, regardless of your behavior, appearance, strengths, or weaknesses, your self-esteem will remain unshakeable.

Self-Preparation
The preparation phase is simple. Take the time to clearly remember what it is like for you to do each of the following:

- Talk on the telephone

- Take a bath or shower

- Eat

- Be angry

- Be happy

- Run

- Fail at something

- Succeed at something

- Be in school

- Be attracted to someone

Next, remember each of the following:

- A time when you were about eight years old

- Your earliest memory

- The last time you were naked

- The last time you wore clothes you really liked

- A time when you wore clothes you really disliked

- Yesterday morning, just after you woke up

- When you believed in Santa Claus (or another childhood belief you no longer have)

- A time when your hair was shorter than it is now

Now, reflect back on these memories. What do they all have in common? The answer is both simple and very important. In each memory there is a YOU; the same you. Your SELF connects all these and any other memories you have. It connects everything you do, think, feel, or believe with every other thing you do, think, feel, or believe. Your behavior changes (talking on the phone is different than taking a shower), your thoughts change (thinking of school is different than thinking of someone to whom you are attracted), your feelings change (feeling sad is different than feeling happy), and your beliefs change (you once believed in Santa Claus or some other childhood fantasy but don't now). Success or failure, it is the same you. Baby, child, teenager, or adult, it is the same you. Stylish clothes or ugly clothes, it is the same you. With acne or without acne, it is the same you; the same SELF. This is the immutable, unchangeable, immeasurable SELF that is you. The SELF that is you is a completely perfect, undefileable creation. When this simple truth finally takes hold, esteem for this SELF is the only natural state.

Physical Preparations

Your working space will need to be private and warm, as you will not have any clothes on for part of this ritual. You will wear only four articles of clothing at the beginning and again at the end of the ritual. Choose them for comfort and ease of removal (for example, sweatpants, sweatshirt, undershirt, and underpants). If you have ritual clothing that you normally wear when casting spells, then include them, but limit the total number of articles to four. Purify any of the clothes not normally reserved for casting spells.

Ritual

Cast and cleanse your circle, and face east. Speak the following words from memory:

> *This ritual, enacted to reveal the immutable aspect of my true nature, is well and truly begun.*

Proclaim your intention.

Ascend to your higher state.

Face west, and remove your first garment. Hold *Foundations of Magic,* and read the following words with force and conviction:

> **In the sanctity of this circle I temporarily discard the garment of my feelings and emotions. My heart I make peaceful. My passions and sentiments I calm. I enter the Western halcyon.**

Turn slowly clockwise to face north.

Remove your second garment. Hold this book, and read the following words with force and conviction:

> **In the sanctity of this circle I temporarily discard the garments of my actions and of my appearance. My body I make still and unseen. My movements and images I calm. I enter the Northern halcyon.**

Slowly turn clockwise to face east.

Remove your third garment. Hold this book, and read the following words with force and conviction:

In the sanctity of this circle I temporarily discard the garments of my thoughts. My mind I make still. My ideas and opinions I put to one side. I enter the Eastern halcyon.

Slowly turn clockwise to face south.

Remove your last garment. Hold this book, and read the following words with force and conviction:

In the sanctity of this circle I temporarily discard the garments of my power. I abandon both vulnerability and strength. My inner forces and outer energies I allay. I enter the Southern halcyon.

Slowly turn clockwise and once again face west. Read the following words forcefully and with building volume and tempo:

Naked within the protective sanctity of my circle am I.
Pure I.
Immutable I.
The I of any feelings or no feelings.
The I of many actions and appearances or no actions and without appearance.
The I of thoughts and ideas and the I of none.
The I of strength and vulnerability and the I of neither strength nor
    vulnerability.
The I of past, present and future.
I am my self the immutable aspect of my true nature.
I am my self unassailable.
I am my self transcendent of measure and value.
I am my self the absolute essence of the esteemed.
I am my self the observer.
I observe my self and learn.

Remain silent for several minutes and reflect upon your SELF. Be aware of your nakedness. Notice what you are learning.

Slowly turn counterclockwise and face south.

Don the last garment you removed. Read the following words with force and conviction:

> I reclaim my power, for it drives and directs the forces in and around me and is a valued but transient aspect of my life. It exists in ever present contrast to MY SELF, the esteemed and immutable aspect of my true nature.

Slowly turn counterclockwise to face east.

Don the third garment you removed. Read the following words with force and conviction:

> I reclaim my thoughts and ideas, for they weave the fabric of meaning and understanding and are a valued but transient aspect of my life. They exist in ever-present contrast to MY SELF, the esteemed and immutable aspect of my true nature.

Slowly turn counterclockwise to face north.

Don the second garment you removed. Read the following words with force and conviction:

> I reclaim my actions and appearances, for they are beautifully varied in their purpose and effect and are a valued but transient aspect of my life. They exist in ever-present contrast to MY SELF, the esteemed and immutable aspect of my true nature.

Slowly turn counterclockwise to face west.

Don the first garment you removed. Read the following words with force and conviction:

I reclaim my feelings and emotions, for they are rich in texture and are a valued but transient aspect of my life. They exist in ever-present contrast to MY SELF, the esteemed and immutable aspect of my true nature.

Now my Will be done,
And with everything I've Willed,
Harm will come to none,
As this purpose is fulfilled.

Descend from your higher state.

Disperse your circle. LET GO and allow the magic to work.

INCREASING PERSONAL POWER

This spell works on two simple and powerful principles. The first is that any purpose can be achieved through the power of Will. The second principle is that the full strength of our own personal power is always present. We need only recognize it. Only a short spell is required.

Self-Preparation

As discussed in chapter 1, true power is power through, not power over. Take some time to reflect on your desire to increase your personal power. What are your motives? What do you think it would be like to experience the full strength of your personal power? Are there any ways in which you are confusing true personal power with power over? It is important that you are clear in your motives and ideas about power. If your desire is for power over, this spell will be rendered ineffective.

Physical Preparations

Place a stand in the center of the area where you will be casting your circle.

Ritual

Cast and cleanse your circle, and face east.

Proclaim your intention.

Ascend to your higher state and recite the following words from memory with force and conviction:

> *I now commence with this ritual of power,*
> *Not of power over but of power through.*

Read the following words with the full force of your Will. From your higher state, be fully mindful of your personal power. Be mindful that you cannot diminish your power;

you can only fail to recognize it. Direct the message to yourself and to the universe as if you are announcing your magic:

> Cast away those obstacles in my mind and intellect that bind me back from my own strength of Will and action. Strengthen those aspects of mind and intellect that are allied with the true nature of my power.

Face **south** and read the following words, again being mindful of the same things:

> Cast away those obstacles to my courage that bind me back from my own strength of Will and action. Strengthen those aspects of my fortitude that are allied with the true nature of my power.

Face **west** and read the following words, again being mindful of the same things:

> Cast away those obstacles in my emotions, intuition and sensuality that bind me back from my own strength of Will and action. Strengthen those aspects of emotion, intuition and sensuality that are allied with the true nature of my power.

Face **north** and read the following words, again being mindful of the same things:

> Cast away those obstacles in my quest for survival that bind me back from my own strength of Will and action. Strengthen those aspects of my material world and my survival instinct that are allied with the true nature of my power.

Again, face **east** and read the following words. As you do, open your arms out in front of you and feel the embrace of your own power:

> The power that is my birthright come through me;
> In this matter my Will shall be done;
> 'Tis the power to serve me and thee;
> And harm shall come to none.

Descend from your higher state.

Disperse your circle.

Follow-up

For a while, forget about power. LET GO and allow the magic to work. In a short time you will realize that you are doing things differently.

RESOLVING
PERSISTENT PROBLEMS
(New Ways to Derive Benefits and Meet Needs)

This spell can be used to resolve longstanding personal problems. These are problems that have persisted because, along with the trouble they bring, they also bring benefits or serve basic needs. Before working this spell, it may be useful to review the section in chapter 2 on "Problems, Unconscious Parts, and Benefits," starting on page 33.

Self-Preparation

The following exercise is very similar to Exercise 1 in chapter 2 (page 37). Write down a brief description of your problem on one side of a full-size piece of white parchment. On the other side, write the following title at the top: "Services, Benefits and Needs."

Enter a light to medium trance. Now, imagine the unconscious part of you that is in charge of this problem. Get in touch with this part in some intuitive way. If you have difficulty doing this, just pretend that you are in communication with the part. As odd as it may seem, genuinely thank that part for its intention to serve you so faithfully with benefits. Ask that part if it will reveal what those intended benefits are.

Now, on the parchment, list the benefits that this part is intending to provide or the needs it is attempting to meet. As before, if you don't think you know, make up some answers. Spend as much time as you need to feel intuitively that you have a complete list.

Physical Preparations

Place the parchment you have written on (above), along with a fountain pen (or brush and ink), on a stand located in the center of the area in which you will cast your circle. During the ritual you will be instructed to draw a pentagram on the parchment. A pentagram is simply a five-pointed star and should be drawn in the manner illustrated below.

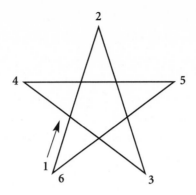

Ritual

Cast and cleanse your circle, and face east.

Proclaim your intention.

Ascend to your higher state.

Hold up the parchment with your arms extended out in front of you, holding it with your right hand at top of the page and your left hand at the bottom. Turn the side with the list of benefits away from you so that it is facing out to the periphery of your circle, and the side with the description of the problem is facing you.

Read the following words out loud:

> Magic of the east, I Will thee draw from this list what is of intellect and of mind and from what thou appropriate, form the means for the consummation of the union of these things and my true nature. Work in concert as one aspect within the quadrinity of Cardinal powers.

Face south and read the following words out loud:

> Magic of the south, I Will thee draw from this list what is of change and courage and from what thou appropriate, form the means for the consummation of the

union of these things and my true nature. Work in concert as one aspect within the quadrinity of Cardinal powers.

Face west and read the following words out loud:

Magic of the west, I Will thee draw from this list what is of emotion and intuition and from what thou appropriate, form the means for the consummation of the union of these things and my true nature. Work in concert as one aspect within the quadrinity of Cardinal powers.

Face north and read the following words out loud:

Magic of the north, I Will thee draw from this list what is of the body and of survival and from what thou appropriate, form the means for the consum0mation of the union of these things and my true nature. Work in concert as one aspect within the quadrinity of Cardinal powers.

Slowly turn clockwise on your own axis for one revolution; as you turn, read the following words:

Magic of the four directions of cardinal power, I Will thee work in concert to open my eyes and my heart and my mind and to clear my path to spiritual ascension in all matters pertaining to what is written upon this parchment.

Face east again, and fold the parchment twice, once along its length and once along its width, so that it is folded in quarters. With the brush or pen, draw the pentagram, a symbol of protection, on each side of the folded parchment. It's alright if the pentagram is drawn on top of the words you have written. Hold the parchment out in front of you in your right hand, and read the following words out loud:

Will that the matters written about on this parchment are at the affect of none but the magic of the four cardinal powers, which I have called upon to do my bidding, and be addressed in concordance with my own true nature and free Will. Make it so with harm to none.

Descend from your higher state.

Disperse your circle.

Follow-up

Carry the parchment with you for the remainder of the day and place it under your pillow at night. Continue to carry it with you (in your pocket, purse, pack, etc.) by day and place it under your pillow at night for a total of twenty-two days and nights. Briefly be aware of the parchment before you fall asleep at night, for it is during sleep that this magic is strongest. At the same time, remember to LET GO and let the magic work. Also, do not be concerned if the parchment becomes ripped or tattered, as this is just an indication that it is being actively used. At the end of the twenty-two days, respectfully burn the parchment, being aware as you do, that the benefits are now yours without the problem.

FINDING A LOST ITEM

All things are exactly where they should be and are therefore never really lost—they are only lost to you. If something is lost to you, then you must reestablish a connection with it in order to locate it. This spell establishes the reconnection quite efficiently, though not always exactly on your schedule.

Self-Preparation

Enter a light to medium trance. Once you have achieved a trance state, make the item as real as you can within your own mind. Picture it as if you are looking right at it. Touch it and feel its contours and textures. Hear any noise it may make, or even what it would sound like if you were to tap your fingers against it. Remember what it smells like. Even if it is something that you don't necessarily associate with having a scent—for example, a key—imagine holding it close to your nose and sniffing it to smell whatever faint odor exists. Do the same with taste. Let your mind fully know this lost item. When you are complete with this mental exercise, come out of trance.

Physical Preparations

Place a stand where you plan to cast your circle.

Ritual

Cast and cleanse your circle, and face east, with the stand in front of you.

Proclaim your intention.

Ascend to your higher state. From your higher state, repeat the exercise you performed while in trance during the Self-Preparation phase. Once again, make the item as real as you can within your own mind. Using all of your senses, let your mind fully know this lost item. Recite the following words with a sense of mischievousness. Project the words in a manner that conveys confidence that you will soon find the item regardless of where it is hiding.

I smell you thing
I taste you thing
I hear you thing
I see you thing
I feel you thing
I possess you in my mind

I play my game
I call your name

I put you somewhere down
And now I look around
But all the while
With an inward smile
I know you're already found

And now I let the matter be
For in due time you'll come to me

Descend from your higher state.

Disperse your circle. LET GO and allow the magic to work.

NOT TAKING YOURSELF OR YOUR SITUATION SO SERIOUSLY

People tend to take themselves too seriously when they are dealing with a persistent or major problem. The difficulty in taking things too seriously is that it starts rendering you ineffective. You start identifying with the problem rather than with the rest of life. Your perspective narrows, and attempts to solve the problem tend to focus on only one course. Many possible solutions and approaches are lost due to this narrowing of attention. To make things worse, you don't have any fun. This is a great spell to cast whenever you find yourself in such a state. It relies heavily on the magic inherent in humor.

Self-Preparation

An imagination game is needed to prime you for this spell. Think of someone you know and respect, someone you trust and who has a good sense of humor and a ready laugh. Visualize this person as if you were with them and something incredibly funny was just said or done. Picture this person uncontrollably laughing really hard. Hear their laughter in your mind. Take the time to fully create this experience in your imagination.

Next, imagine that some days later you are having a serious conversation with this same person. In your mind, relate the details of your problem or situation. When you have finished, imagine that this person finds your whole story just as funny as what was said or done in the exercise above. Again, picture this person and hear them laughing uncontrollably, only this time at the story of your problem or situation. Once again, fully create this experience.

Because of the unusual vocabulary found in this spoken verse, take special care in familiarizing yourself with it before you attempt to read it aloud.

Physical Preparations

Place a hand mirror on a stand in the center of the location where you plan to cast your circle.

Ritual

Cast and cleanse your circle, and face east.

Proclaim your intention.

Ascend to your higher state. Read the following verse in a very solemn voice:

> The world is such a phlare de wern;
> I understand non tune mineshern.
> bol wills is swarmly consummate,
> But only if dalval can milipate.
> Flish-on, Flish-on: don't blandly Zon;
> Co-findle will bring you much applephon.
> Applephon, applephon, lillysnout;
> What, praise the lord, am I talking about?
>
> My big concern is swinglee rowe;
> I fear she cal na-tu, na-tu.
> If true, sam willy willy ho ho,
> Nol tube swine zero shall We do?
>
> Oh how can I go on, go on,
> With problems so very quizzical?
> My life's a big messy bon bon,
> and I have no idea what I isical.
>
> I know what will make my problems abate!
> fret, fear, deny, accept, blame, pet the dog, hate,
> weep, scorn, argue, eat, lie, fish, masturbate,
> shame, condemn, fight, run, self flagellate,
> forgive, dismiss, sleep, drink booze, procreate,
> get a high colonic, shop, gamble, manipulate,
> pray, confess, watch football, work, go on a date,
> infuriate, capitulate, urinate, defecate, celebrate,
> but wait!
> This could go on like this until it becomes very late.

This rimy side climble is hopeless it would seem;
It doesn't even stay with the same rhyming scheme.
So I dismiss all these quachits with bold counterstrokes,
and instead I'll go looking for some really good jokes.
With certainty I know where the first jest will be,
as I hold up the looking glass and there: BEHOLD ME!

Hold up the mirror to view yourself. Laugh if so inclined.

Descend from your higher state.

Disperse your circle. LET GO, smile, and let the magic work.

RESOLVING UNCOMFORTABLE SITUATIONS
(Breaking Old Patterns)

Everybody has recurring situations that consistently result in a feeling of discomfort or even mild fear. It may be talking to your boss, phoning your mother, talking in front of a group, or going to the dentist. Exactly what constitutes an uncomfortable situation is different for each person. The problem with the discomfort is that it often results in us avoiding something to which we need to attend, and when we finally do attend to it, the experience is unpleasant. This spell will eliminate the discomfort for any given situation, but you must be quite specific about just what situation you are considering.

Self-Preparation

The Self-Preparation phase of this spell is somewhat lengthy and very important to the spell's success. Be thorough. For the purposes of brevity, the uncomfortable situation you choose will be referred to as the "situation" in the rest of this text.

Before you begin this section, prepare the two symbols as described in the Physical Preparations section below. Place the symbols in the working space in front of you with the situation symbol on the right and the truth aspect symbol on the left.

Enter a light to medium trance. Remember three specific instances of being in the situation. It is important that each instance is a specific event and not just a vague feeling of past situations. Relive the first event, making it as real as possible. Get in touch with the uncomfortable feelings. When you are in touch with the feelings, place the palm of your right hand on the situation (black) symbol. Hold your hand on the symbol for the entire period you experience the uncomfortable feelings, and remove it when you are ready to move on to the next memory. Repeat this sequence for the remaining two memories. If you have any difficulty experiencing these feelings, review the section on memories in chapter 2, page 42. If you are still experiencing difficulty, invoke the Law of Pretending.

When you have completed reliving the three specific memories of the situation, remove your hand from the situation symbol for the last time. Now, think of something completely unrelated for a minute or two, until you are completely out of the experience of being in the situation.

Next, reflect on what you would like to experience in the situation, instead of the uncomfortable feelings. For instance, if you are nervous and distracted every time you call your mother, perhaps you would prefer to be relaxed and alert. This positive experience will be referred to as your truth aspect. When you choose a truth aspect be sure you choose something that is actually beneficial and is consistent with your true nature. Don't mistake truth with force or dominance. In this example, notice that the truth aspect is a relaxed alertness with no implication of force.

Just about any appropriate truth aspect you choose is one that you already posses in some other area of your life, an area that has nothing to do with the situation. This is true of everybody. For example, there are almost certainly times in your life when you feel relaxed and alert. It may be reading a good book in the bathtub, gardening, fishing or any number of other circumstances. Remember three different times in your life when you experienced your truth aspect. The memories may be of three different times of doing the same activity, or they may all be three different activities in which you experience this truth aspect. As with your three memories of the situation, it is important that each instance is a specific event and not just a vague feeling of past experiences. With each memory, get in touch with the feeling of your truth aspect (in the example above, this would be the feelings of relaxed alertness). When you are in touch with the feelings, place the palm of your left hand on the truth aspect (yellow) symbol. Hold your hand on the symbol for the entire period you experience the feelings, and remove it when you are ready to move on to the next memory. When you are finished getting in touch with the feelings of the last memory, remove your hand from the truth aspect symbol and come out of trance.

This ritual is full of small details (for instance, in directing when which hand is to go where). You are advised to carefully read the ritual instructions below, and practice them enough times to allow you to execute them smoothly during the ritual.

Physical Preparations

Prepare two symbols, one for your old uncomfortable responses in the situation, and one for your new truth aspect responses. You will need a piece of black paper and a piece of yellow paper. Draw a 2-inch diameter circle on each piece of paper, using a compass or a round object of that size to trace it. Cut out each circle with care. Then, using a fountain pen with black ink, write a brief description of your old responses on the black circle. Write in the past tense. The description can be a simple as, for example, "I was nervous and distracted." The black ink will be difficult or impossible to see on the black paper, but this is as it should be. On the yellow paper, write a brief description of your truth aspect responses, once again in black ink. Write this in the present tense, for example, "I am relaxed and alert."

After having used the two symbols in the Self-Preparation phase, place them about 18 to 24 inches apart on a stand in the center of the area where you will cast your circle. This time, place the black circle on the left and the yellow circle on the right. Place this book open on the stand, so that you may read it without holding it, but do not place it between the two symbols.

Ritual
Cast and cleanse your circle, and face east.

Proclaim your intention.

Enter a light to medium trance.

Place the palm of your right hand on the black symbol by reaching across to the left side of the stand. With your hand in this position recite the following words from memory:

> *This is my way before*
> *This is my way of yore*
> *This shall be no more*

Relive the three past memories of the situation. Just as you did in Self-Preparation, fully experience these specific events from your past. Experience them one by one in the same order you did in the Self-Preparation exercise. Again, get in touch with the feelings of discomfort. All the while, keep your right hand on the black symbol of your old discomfort.

Turn clockwise on your own axis, and again face east. When you are finished reliving the three experiences, remove your right hand from the symbol, look up, and turn a complete circle clockwise on your own axis (staying on the same spot). While you are turning recite the following words from memory:

Turn from old ways
Turn from past days
Without further delays

Place the palm of your left hand on the yellow symbol by reaching across to the right side of the stand. With your hand in this position recite the following words from memory:

This is my way anew
This is my nature true
This is my way overdue

Relive the three memories of your truth aspect. Just as you did in Self-Preparation, fully experience these specific events from your past. Experience them one by one in the same order you did in the beginning exercise. Again, get in touch with the feelings of your truth aspect. All the while, keep the palm of your left hand on the yellow symbol.

Turn clockwise on your own axis. When you are finished reliving the three experiences of your truth aspect, remove your left hand from the symbol, look up, and turn a complete a circle clockwise on your own axis. While you are turning, recite the following words from memory:

Turn to the new
Turn to the true
The old ways eschew

Cross your hands over the symbols. With your right hand, reach to the left and again place your palm on the black symbol. Leaving your right hand in place over the black symbol, reach under your right arm with your left hand, and place your palm on the yellow symbol of your truth aspect. Your arms are now crossed in front of you with your right arm over your left arm.

Move the two symbols together. Very slowly slide your two hands, along with the two symbols, toward the middle, ending up with both symbols under your left hand (with your right hand on top of your left hand). Lift your right hand up and leave your left hand over both symbols while you recite the following words from memory. Speak with firm conviction. Keep your hand on the symbols for several minutes while the magic woks. Use your magical sense or intuition to know how long this should be.

> *Now my Will be done*
> *Let the magic work*
> *And harm shall come to none*

Come back up out of trance.

Disperse your circle.

Follow-up
After you close your circle, clip or tape the two symbols securely together, and put them in a safe place. Forget about them, LET GO, and allow the magic to work.

CHANGING YOUR SELF-IMAGE

This spell is intended for those who have a poor self-image. This should not be confused with poor self-esteem. Self-image quite literally refers to how people see themselves. There are some people who have both poor self-esteem and poor self-image and would benefit from working both this spell and Realizing Self-Esteem (page 151).

This is a lovely realignment ritual in which self-trickery is dispelled and accuracy restored. It works with the powerful magic that comes from realizing your true self. As with all spells, be sure to be thorough in the Self-Preparation phase.

Self-Preparation

Everyone who has a poor self-image has it for only one reason: they are making an inappropriate comparison. Before you can judge anything, you must compare it with something else. When you look at yourself in the mirror (or when you think of yourself) and don't like what you see, it is because either consciously or, more often, unconsciously you are comparing the image you see with a mental image of some idealized you that doesn't exist. Sometimes the idealized you is an altered, stylized version of how you already look. Sometimes the idealized you will look more like someone else—perhaps a friend, a model, or someone else you admire. Often, there is more than one idealized image. You may, for instance, approve of your eyes and your hair, but compare your nose to your image of an idealized nose, your ears to some idealized ears, and your mouth to some idealized mouth.

No matter what you are like, if you compare yourself with an image of what you are not like, you will always be disappointed. This is pure self-trickery. You are tricking yourself into thinking that you can look like the false image, and worse, you are tricking yourself that you should look like the false image.

To prepare for this spell, attempt to get in touch with your false image or images. Look in a mirror or simply think of yourself and how you look. Ask yourself, "How do I know that this isn't exactly how I should look? What makes the image of me, as I am, not completely perfect?" In order to accurately answer these questions you will have to form a mental comparison image. Play with this until you are conscious of what comparisons you are making. If you have difficultly bringing the false comparison images into consciousness, then pay attention to your feelings and word-thoughts and invoke the Law of Pretending. Pretend you are aware of your false images.

Hold your arms outstretched in front of you, with the palms of your hands facing toward you. Position your hands so that they are about three-feet apart and a foot above the level of your head. Keep your head facing directly forward. Move your eyes (not your head) to look up at your right palm, and think of your false images. Next, look at your left palm and think of your false images, once again, without moving your head. Which palm intuitively feels like the right place to view your comparison image? For most people, one palm will simply feel like the "right" one. In fact, some people will only be able to visualize the image on one side. If you do not notice any difference, then once again pretend you do, and choose a side: right or left. For the purposes of this spell, the side you choose will be referred to as your comparison side.

Physical Preparations

Prepare a six-by-six inch parchment symbol of your false image. This is done by thinking of your false image and drawing a representation of it on the parchment. There does not have to be any artistic value to this drawing. Within your abilities, simply draw some image that symbolizes your false comparison image. If you have more than one false image, then draw the one you feel is most characteristic, recognizing that this represents all of your false images.

In addition to the parchment with the symbol drawn on it, you will require two hand mirrors, a full-length mirror, a lit white or yellow candle, a ceramic saucer or plate, and a chair. Place the two hand mirrors, the parchment, and the lighted candle on a stand located in the center of the area where you will cast your circle. Place the chair on the east side of the stand, about four feet away. The back of the chair should be facing toward the stand. Lean the full-length mirror against the back of the chair, so that when you are in front of it you can see all of yourself.

Choose one of the two hand mirrors as your comparison mirror, and when you pick it up during the ritual, hold it with the hand that is on your comparison side. The other mirror will be referred to as your "memory" mirror and will be held in the other hand.

Ritual

Cast and cleanse your circle, and face east.

Proclaim your intention.

Ascend to your higher state and face west. You should be positioned between the stand and the full-length mirror, facing the stand with your back to the mirror. Recite the following words from memory:

Imagery
Of three times me
Reverse
The curse
Of self trickery

Hold up the parchment symbol of the false image with the hand on your comparison side. With your arm outstretched, hold it slightly off to one side and about a foot above your head level, as you did with your palm in the Self-Preparation exercise. Hold this book in the other hand, and read the following words.

This is the symbol of the false images of me which is not of me nor of my true nature and is created from the influences of others who know not of my true nature nor understand me fully nor understand the nature of human perfection which derives from the One source of all perfection of which I am a perfect manifestation, and this is the last time I look to this symbol of the false image of me; nevermore to believe it, nor strive to simulate it, nor to find merit in it, nor to be desirous of it, nor to associate it with me and forevermore to rid myself of its sight and its useless burden and its unnatural and corrupted portrayal of mistaken visions.

Review the false image or images in your mind's eye.

Ignite the parchment in the candle flame and let it burn out on the saucer or plate. As it burns, visualize all of the old comparison images distorting and disappearing just as the parchment symbol is. When it has completely burnt to ashes, say the words:

Imagery
Of three times me

Dispel the spell
Of inadequacy

Pick up the two hand mirrors, and face east, looking toward the full-length mirror. Hold the hand mirrors out in front of you, one in each hand about three feet apart and a foot above the level of your head (similar to the way you positioned your palms during the Self-Preparation exercise). Hold the comparison mirror on your comparison side and the memory mirror on the other side. Keep your head facing directly toward the full-length mirror.

Look first at the full-length mirror. Then, without moving your head, move only your eyes and look at the memory mirror in your hand. Next, look at your comparison image mirror. You will repeat this sequence—full-length mirror, memory mirror, comparison mirror—over and over. Each time you change your glance to a different mirror, pause very briefly to focus on your image and then shift your eyes and look at the next mirror. Repeat this 10 or 15 times as you recite the following words. The timing of the words should correspond to the mirror you are looking at, as indicated in the brackets.

Imagery
of three times me
This is me I see [full-length mirror]
This is me in memory [memory mirror]
This is me as I ought to be [comparison mirror]

Stop and gaze at yourself in the full-length mirror, and notice if you look just as you should at this moment. If not, then repeat the process, along with the above recitation, until you do (you may have to reposition the mirrors so that you are seeing a different part of yourself in order to bring all of your new comparison image into alignment with your true self). This is strong magic and the moment when you see your true self always comes soon. When it does, recite the following words:

Self Imagery
Of me times three
Magically and irrevocably

Dispelled the spell
Of inadequacy,
& reversed
The curse
Of self trickery.
So mote it be!

Descend from your higher state.

Disperse your circle.

Follow-up

Take the ashes of the burnt parchment and sprinkle them at the base of a favorite houseplant or shrub. Feel content that the symbol of past troubles is finally bringing benefit by providing food for a plant friend.

After you have lived with a good self-image for a while you may find that there are some reasonable changes that you would like to make. Perhaps you would like to adjust your posture, lose or gain some weight, adopt a new hairstyle, or any number of other changes. You can proceed with making these changes from an entirely different perspective than from that of your old, poor self-image. You can approach these changes from the perspective of achieving an interesting goal rather than correcting some deficiency.

If there are changes you desire, keep them realistic and attainable. Check your motives. Make sure you are doing this for your own sense of creativity and enjoyment. One of the best tests of your motives is to ask yourself, "What if I don't make these changes?" If your answer is something like, "it doesn't much matter," then you are probably on the right track. It is also important to attempt any changes in small steps. For instance, if you wish to loose twenty pounds, first picture yourself only five pounds lighter and aim for that goal. If you reach that goal, then picture yourself a further five pounds lighter. This way your goal for the future and where you are now are never very far apart.

ELIMINATING DEPRESSION OR THE BLUES

Many traditional elements of Hermetic magic are interwoven in the design of this spell, including the words of the great Hermes himself. This is a very powerful ritual, and will prove especially effective in amplifying the effects of more conventional treatments for your malaise.

Self-Preparation

Many people who are feeling really down have a difficult time accomplishing necessary everyday tasks. There is no need to aggravate this situation by adding more things for you to do before the rapid road to recovery begins. For this reason, the Self-Preparation task is simple and takes little time. Most of what will be required of you is the aerial search that follows the casting of this spell.

Take two or three minutes to imagine what your life will be like when you are free of the blues and things are looking up. Begin casting your spell immediately after you have done this.

Physical Preparation

Place a stand on the southern edge of the area where you plan to cast your circle. When the circle is cast, the center must be free of objects.

Instead of using the usual rosemary tea, you will cleanse and purge your circle with an incense of St. John's Wort. This herb, which has gained such notoriety as of late, has many ancient and powerful uses in magic. It is available in either dried or powdered form at most health food stores and pharmacies. Place a lit candle, incense holder, and incense charcoal on the stand prior to casting your circle. Take about a teaspoon of the St. John's Wort from its original package (this may involve removing the powder from a capsule) and put it on the stand, on a piece of parchment, or in a special container of your choosing.

Ritual

Cast your circle and cleanse with incense, and face east. Use the following procedure. Light the charcoal with the candle just after casting your circle. Once the charcoal is lit, place several pinches of the St. John's Wort on it. If your incense holder is the type that is suspended from wires or chains and can be swung (a censer), then swing it three times toward the east as you recite the following words. If it is a holder that cannot be swung, then raise it up and down three times as you recite:

> *With the power and protection of this elevating herb I cleanse the [Eastern] domain.*

Repeat this for each of the remaining three cardinal directions, substituting the name for the appropriate direction each time.

Proclaim your intention.

Get in touch with your blues. Take a minute to quietly review your down experiences. Make no effort to resist feeling the deepest shade of blue you can reach. Take this book in your left hand, and hold it down in front of you a little lower than waist level. Let your right arm fall loosely at your side. The position is important.

Read the words within the frame. They are words from Hermes Trismegistus and are inscribed in the legendary Emerald Tablet. Read them as you would proclaim an inviolable law.

What is below is like that which is above,
and what is above is like that which is below,
to accomplish the miracles of one thing . . .

Ascend with the greatest sagacity from the earth to heaven,
and then again descend to earth,
and join together the powers of things superior and inferior.
Thus you will obtain the glory of all the world . . .

Read the following words with **somber conviction** and forceful determination, as if the words originated inside you:

> I shall use this truth writ upon the plaque,
> By Wise Hermes the Thrice Great,
> To find deliverance from my humor so black,
> And my anguished suffering to ameliorate.
>
> Too long I have attended to things below,
> And too long have my eyes looked down;
> I now lift my gaze skyward, apropos,
> Of my sagacious ascent to the crown.

Ascend to your higher state. As you ascend, shift your eyes from looking down to looking up to the heavens. Raise this book, so that it is held out in front of you, and raise your right arm, so that your outstretched hand is held above eye level. Read the following words with a firm and resolute tone:

> 'Tis here where Hermes' magic first comes in;
> Magic of scarlet and crimson and red;
> For upon leaving this circle my quest will begin,
> For a ruby vision of solace seen overhead.
> High magic of colors that dwell in the sky,
> I Will thee to work on my behest;
> Recruit the emissary of red as my ally;
> Let me recognize when it does manifest.

Descend from your higher state.

Disperse your circle.

Follow-up

This short, powerful spell sets many things in motion, both within you and out in the universe. Your task now is to recognize when all the necessary adjustments have been made, so as to complete the alleviation of your blues. The completion will be marked by some vision of red, which you will see manifest above you. This will not be an imaginary vision of red, rather it will be something you actually see. It could be anything you catch a glimpse of that is both red and visible above you. Examples could be the lettering on a sign, a helicopter, a red piece of trim on a building, a red light fixture, or a stripe of red on a flag.

There is a very interconnected process at work here (and it does not make any kind of rational sense, so do not waste energy trying to figure it out). You will not recognize the right vision of red until all the necessary magical changes have been brought about. Once the changes are made, you will not experience their full effect until you recognize the vision. Searching for the vision will speed up the changes. You must be vigilant. Frequently look up at the things around you. When you see it, you will know.

If you have been depressed for any longer than a week or two, remember the Law of Prudence, and be sure that you seek out the help of a professional in addition to working this spell.

ELIMINATING A PHOBIA

This spell is designed to eliminate phobias. Strong fear and phobias are not always the same. A phobia is a strong, full-body fear of some specific stimulus. Someone who is truly phobic will have the response even at the thought of the stimulus. For instance, if someone says to you, "I'm really afraid of spiders," ask them, "What would you do if there was a spider on you at this very moment?" If they have a fully fearful response right then and there at that suggestion, then they are phobic. If they simply tell you that they would be extremely frightened, but exhibit no significant indication of fear, then they are not phobic. If, rather than a phobia, you have a strong fear of something or some situation, then consider working the spell Increasing Personal Power (page 157) or Resolving Uncomfortable Situations (page 169).

When you cast this spell, you will have the opportunity to reverse time in magical time-space and to make certain adjustments which may not appear to be at all rational, but which are all that is needed to undo a phobia. You will also be able to experience a version of astral travel, where you can leave the circle in your imagination and be in more than one place at the same time.

The procedure for this spell is fairly complicated and will require more study and practice than most. Once you cast this spell, let your imagination take over to work its magic.

Self-Preparation

Remember a past situation in which you had your strongest phobic response. You do not have to remember it so well that you experience it, just have the memory ready for working the spell. If no single incident stands out as stronger than another, pick a specific past phobia situation you remember clearly. For convenience, this past situation will be referred to as "the event" in the instructions that follow.

Ready your imagination for the experience of astral traveling and being in several places at once. (You may wish to review the brief section on astral travel in chapter 1, page 20.) Imagine for the moment that you are looking at a photograph of yourself sitting on a warm beach. Now imagine that you drift out of, and a short distance away from, your body, so that you can see yourself looking at the photo. Now, there are two "yous," the "you" who is looking at the photo, and the "you" looking at the "you" who is looking at the photo. Plus, there is an image of you in the photo.

Drift back into your first body and again be the "you" looking at the photo. Now, leave this body and drift into the photograph and be the "you" in the photo. Once again there are two "yous," but this time it is the "you" looking at the photo and the "you" in the photo. Practice shifting between these three different perspectives.

There may be a small aspect of your old phobia that is valuable, even if you are not consciously aware of it. For example, a phobia of heights can prevent you from doing something completely foolish, such as walking on an upper window ledge of a high building. In designing your intention, be sure to include a desire to keep any valuable aspects of your phobia. For example, if you have a fear of heights, you could state your intention "to be free of an irrational fear of heights."

Physical Preparations

Place a chair and a stand in the center of the location where you plan to cast your circle. Have the chair facing east.

Ritual

Cast and cleanse your circle, and face east.

Proclaim your intention.

Ascend to your higher state. Read the following words. Speak firmly and project well. You are directing this out into the universe and you want the words to be clearly heard. Read with conviction as, if every word originated from within you:

> **The clock is our ally,**
> **In a widely agreed upon lie,**
> **That time goes in sequence,**
> **Round its fixed circumference.**
>
> **But beyond the mortal realm,**
> **'Tis another order at the helm,**
> **Where words have no tense,**
> **For 'tis NOW that has eminence.**

Future, present, past,
What is first is also last.
Time is all of one,
What's over has not begun.

But the psyche of our mortal coil,
Must reject such temporal turmoil,
So a structure we impose on time,
And take comfort in the hourly chime.

Now 'twixt time caged and time true,
Events can form which go askew,
And from the temporal firmament,
Can occur vexatious mis-alignment.

Phobia's fear is born in this way;
A mistaken fear, and easy to allay,
For all that's required to bid fright farewell,
Is that time be reversed for just a short spell.

Sit down in the chair and prepare to astral travel. Imagine that your astral body, including your consciousness, leaves the circle and travels to the location of the Akashic Records.[4] This is an infinite picture gallery of images recording all knowledge of humankind's past, present, and future. The Records are displayed as images, similar to photographs hung in a gallery.

Find the Record of the event. You travel directly to a specific record of your past, the image of you during the event. It is a faded black and white picture, like an old photograph. Take a good look at this picture of you at this past time (when you experienced

---

4. Many Western esoteric traditions teach that magical transformation, including the magic in these spells, is manifested first in the astral plane. The astral plane is a realm of imagination and unembodied consciousness; a place where your physical body can never go. Nevertheless, events that occur there are reported to have a profound effect on a person's life. One of the regions in the astral plane, the region of astral light, is where the Akashic Records are said to exist.

the event). The image is small enough, faded enough, and far enough from you that seeing this image of you being frightened does not affect you.

Have your consciousness drift back to your physical body in the circle. You are now in two places at once. Your astral body is still at the Akashic Records looking at the image of the event. And your consciousness is back inside your physical body in the circle. You can see the astral "you" looking at the photo image of the past "you" in the event. Remember that this is magical time-space, so regardless of how far you seem to have traveled to get to the Akashic Records, they are still within viewing distance of your magic circle. Be aware of the complete protection from all negative forces or experiences you have inside your circle. Know that this protection extends to your astral body.

Activate the Record. Now, when a record is activated, it changes from a still picture to a black and white moving picture—similar to an older television. From within your circle, watch your astral self watching the entire moving picture of the event. There are now essentially three "yous"—the physical "you" in the circle, the astral "you" watching the movie of the event, and the past "you" in the movie. (Any stressful responses your astral self is experiencing while watching your past self in the movie will soon be neutralized with "time reversal.") The movie record will stop when it has advanced in time to the point where your phobic response had passed and you were no longer afraid. In other words, you will again be left with a still image of the past "you," but this time a point when the event was completely over.

Reverse time and realign the event. In your imagination, once again have your consciousness leave the circle and astral travel to rejoin your astral body, which has been viewing the record. Once your consciousness joins your astral body, the astral "you" (as a participant) should be looking directly at the image of the past "you." In your astral body, drift up close to this last image of you at the end of the movie. As you approach the image, it will change from black and white to a color image. Enter the image so that instead of looking at the image, you are actually in it, similar to what you imagined in the Self-Preparation exercise. In an instant, the still image will change to a color movie that you are actually in. The movie will start to run very quickly backward in time, just like a video in a VCR on rewind. Remember to stay in the movie as a participant and re-experience the entire event, but backward and greatly speeded up. Stay in the experience until you come to the beginning of the event.

Travel back to your circle in your imagination, when the movie has run backward right to the beginning. Have your consciousness go back to your astral body, and then have your astral body travel back to your circle and rejoin your physical body. You are now completely back in the circle.

Go into a future time in your imagination—to an event where you will likely encounter the stimulus of your old phobia. How do you feel now? If imagining it still makes you a little uncomfortable, repeat the process of being in the movie and reliving the event quickly in reverse time and in color. Do this until you can easily imagine being in the presence of your old phobic stimulus while remaining at ease.

Declare your Will by memorizing and speaking the following words. State them with force and conviction.

> *Be gone all vestiges of undue fear;*
> *With my life never again interfere.*
> *I Will this magic be done and be done,*
> *With no harm to me or any other one.*

Descend from your higher state.

Disperse your circle.

INCREASING YOUR CONFIDENCE

This spell is specifically for people who lack confidence in some area or areas of their life where confidence is needed.

Self-Preparation

Before you begin, prepare the two symbols as described in the Physical Preparations section below. Place the symbols in the working space in front of you, with the non-confidence symbol on the right and the confidence symbol on the left. For brevity, these symbols will be referred to as the NC and the C symbols, respectively, in the remainder of the instructions for this spell.

Most people lack confidence in specific situations. To concentrate the power of this spell, you will need to pick a specific type of situation in which you lack confidence. For example, you may lack confidence at work, school, or while talking to a certain person.

Enter a light to medium trance. Remember three specific instances when you lacked confidence in this type of situation. For instance, if you lack confidence at work, remember three distinct work-related instances when you felt a lack of confidence. It is important that each instance is a specific event and not just a vague feeling of past situations. One by one, relive each of the events, making them as real as possible. With each memory, get in touch with the feelings that go with lack of confidence. When you are in touch with the feelings, place the palm of your right hand on the NC (black) symbol. Hold your hand on the symbol for the entire period you experience the lack of confidence. Remove your hand when you are ready to move on to the next memory. Repeat this sequence for the remaining two memories. If you have any difficulty experiencing these feelings, review the section on memories in chapter 2, page 48. If you are still having difficulty, invoke the Law of Pretending.

Be sure you remove your hand from the NC symbol when you have completed reliving the third memory. Now, think of something completely unrelated for a minute or two, until you are completely out of the experience of lacking confidence.

Next, remember three different times in your life when you experienced all of the confidence you needed. People will occasionally object that they never really feel confident, but this is simply not true. If someone were to ask such a person if they are confident that they can turn the pages of this book, barring extreme physical disability, they would certainly have to answer yes. It is not important what it is that you are confident about, it is only important that you get in touch with three specific memories of being confident. It is best if you think of three completely unrelated memories of three unrelated situations in which you felt very confident. As with your three memories of having a lack of confidence, it is important that each instance is a specific event and not just a vague feeling of past situations. With each memory, get in touch with the feeling of being confident. When you are in touch with the feeling, place the palm of your left hand on the C (white) symbol. Hold your hand on the symbol for the entire period you experience the feelings of confidence. Remove your hand when you are ready to move on to the next memory. When you are finished getting in touch with the feelings of the last memory remove your hand from the C symbol. Come up out of trance.

This ritual is full of small details (for instance, in directing when which hand is to go where). You are advised to carefully read the Ritual instructions below and practice them enough times to allow you to execute them smoothly during the ritual.

Physical Preparations

Prepare two symbols, one for your old, nonconfident responses and one for your confident responses. You will need a piece of black paper and a piece of white paper. Draw a 2-inch diameter circle on each piece of paper, using a compass or a round object of that size to trace it. Cut out each circle with care. Then, using a fountain pen with black ink, write the words: "past lack of confidence" on the black circle. The black ink will be difficult or impossible to see on the black paper, but this is as it should be. On the white paper, write the words "newfound confidence," once again in black ink.

After using the two symbols in the Self-Preparation phase, place them about 18 to 24 inches apart on a stand in the center of the area where you will cast your circle. This time, place the black circle on the left and the white circle on the right. Place this book open on the stand, so that you can read it without holding it, but do not place it between the two symbols.

Ritual

Cast and cleanse your circle, and face east.

Proclaim your intention.

Enter a light to medium trance.

Place the palm of your right hand on the black symbol by reaching across to the left side of the stand. With your hand in this position, recite the following words from memory:

> *One plus one and two times three*
> *Raised to the power of infinity*
> *This is the magic at work for me!*

Relive the three past memories of nonconfidence. Fully experience the three specific events from your past, one by one, in the same order you did in the Self-Preparation exercise. Again, get in touch with the feelings of lacking confidence, keeping your right hand on the black NC symbol all the while. When you are finished reliving the three experiences, remove your right hand from the NC symbol and look up.

Turn clockwise on your own axis and again face east.

Place the palm of your left hand on the white symbol by reaching across to the right side of the stand. With your hand in this position, recite the following words from memory:

> *One plus one and two times three*
> *Raised to the power of infinity*
> *This is the magic at work for me!*

Relive the three memories of confidence. Fully experience these three specific events from your past, one by one, in the same order you did in the Self-Preparation exercise. Again, get in touch with the feelings of being confident, keeping your left hand over the white symbol all the while. When you are finished reliving the three experiences of confidence, remove your left hand from the symbol and look up.

Turn clockwise on your own axis, and again face east.

Cross your hands over the symbols. With your right hand, reach to the left and again place your palm on the black NC symbol. Leaving your right hand on the black symbol, reach under your right arm with your left hand and place your palm on the white C symbol. Your arms are now crossed in front of you with your right arm over your left arm.

Move the two symbols together. Very slowly slide your two hands (along with the two symbols) toward the middle, ending up with both symbols under your left hand and your right hand on top of your left hand. Lift your right hand up and leave your left hand over both symbols while you recite the following words from memory. Speak with firm conviction. After reciting, keep your left hand on the symbols for several minutes while the magic works. Use your magical sense or intuition to know how long this should be.

> *One plus one and two times three*
> *Raised to the power of infinity*
> *This is the magic at work for me!*
> *I Will my Will to make it be*
> *No harm to you, no harm to me!*

Come back out of trance.

Disperse your circle.

Follow-up
After you close your circle, clip or tape the two symbols securely together and put them in a safe place. Forget about them, LET GO, and allow the magic to work.

A BINDING SPELL

This is a protection spell and is directed toward those who would do you harm in any manner. It is the closest thing you will find to a curse in white magic, but it is firmly based on an intention to do no harm. Just as in some of the more enlightened forms of martial arts, the negative energy of an adversary is redirected back to them. Any negative consequences to the recipient of this spell are a direct result of their own doing. You must be very sure of your motives in casting this spell. Using this spell to seek revenge or redress will render it ineffective and perhaps result in trouble for you.

Self-Preparation

Take some time to yourself, and review your feelings and intentions toward the recipient of this spell. This is a time for complete honesty, as there is no one to deceive but yourself. Your intention in casting this spell must be free of desire to do harm. To be effective, this spell does not demand that you are free of anger, animosity, or even retribution. It does, however, require that none of these be part of your intention when casting this spell. In other words you must separate your own negativity from your desire for protection, then you can work your spell based on a true intention to do no harm.

There is a visual metaphor that helps many people accomplish this separation. First, make a mental or written list of your own negative thoughts and desires. Then, visualize each of these as if they have a physical form (a thought-form[5]). Imagine that you have a storage closet and in the closet is a large empty shelf. As a participant (not an observer), feel yourself take each of these negative thought-forms and set them one by one on the shelf. You can then proceed free from the distractions of these negative influences. You can also rest assured that they are there on the shelf for you to reclaim at a later time if you so choose.

---

5. A thought-form is an important concept in many magical traditions. The basic idea is that thoughts, when created and sustained by individual or group Will and other magical forces, become substantive and take on form in the world, as an entity separate from the person or group who created them.

Physical Preparations

Place a ball of string, a pair of scissors or a sharp knife, and a witness symbol on a stand located in the center of the area where you will cast your circle. A witness symbol can be any number of things that are closely associated to the recipient of this spell. A photograph taken within the last few years is ideal. If there are other people in the photo, cut them out before proceeding. Any small item that was once owned or handled by the person will also work. If none of these things are easily available to you then a five-by-five inch square piece of parchment with the person's name written on it will do. If you do not know the recipient's name, then write a description of the person or the situation on the parchment. For instance, if you are receiving disturbing anonymous phone calls, you could write something like, "This parchment is the symbol of the person who has been making unwanted phone calls."

The string (or strong yarn or thread) should be made from a natural fiber. Although not a common household item, strong silk thread is ideal.

Ritual

Cast and cleanse your circle, and face east.

Proclaim your intention.

Ascend to your higher state. Face the direction where you believe the recipient is located. If you are not sure of the person's whereabouts at the time of casting your spell, then face the direction of their home or workplace. If none of this information is available to you, then use your intuition as to what direction to face.

Wrap the witness symbol round and round with the string. Proceed at a moderate but steady rate. If you are wrapping a photo, piece of parchment, or letter, allow the tension on the string to fold or crumple it as it becomes increasingly bound. In your mind, visualize the recipient being similarly wrapped by the bindings of their own negative intentions. Recite the following words as you bind the witness symbol. Muster a feeling of certainty about what you are doing as you speak them.

I speak to thee and bid thee hear,
I wrap thee round and round and round.

With thine own manipulations I thee ensphere,
With thine own entanglements thou art bound.

I speak to thee and bid thee hear,
From the swaddle thou art easily free,
If to this covenant thou dost adhere;
Cease all black thoughts and animosity!

I speak to thee and bid thee hear,
If thou undo what thou hast done,
All thine own bindings will disappear,
And harm will come to none.

Continue wrapping until the symbol is completely bound. If you finish speaking the above words before you are finished wrapping, then repeat them as many times as is necessary. Be thorough in your binding, letting your intuition signal when you are complete. Cut the string, leaving a piece 12 to 18 inches free to securely tie off the bound symbol.

Descend from your higher state.

Disperse your circle.

Follow-up

Put the bound symbol in a safe place. When the time comes that you are free of the recipient's influence, cut the string off the symbol and burn the string. Dispose of the symbol in whatever way seems appropriate.

GETTING RID OF PESTS

A person, animal, insects, weeds, or any other form of pest can be the focus of this supplementary spell. It is a supplementary spell in that it is designed to be worked in conjunction with other actions you are taking to rid yourself of the particular pest. If the pest is a person who intends you harm, then cast A Binding Spell (page 192) as well as this one.

Self-Preparation

People who have struggled to rid themselves of a persistent pest often lose a sense of humor about it. If this applies to you, it is a good indication that you are not operating from a very effective state of mind. Humor as a personal tool in the war against a pest offers a long list of advantages. Humor forces you to periodically shift perspective, an asset in any battle. It makes the whole enterprise more enjoyable and frees an enormous amount of energy that can so easily get locked up in frustration. It is this last advantage, liberating bound-up energy, which makes humor particularly valuable in working this magic.

Your task in preparing yourself to work this spell is to find three funny things about having this pest in your life. If you are too close to the problem to see where the humor lies (and it is always there somewhere), then talk about your plight with a friend who has a good sense of humor. Your friend will likely see the jokes hidden to you. When you have your three funny things, choose the very funniest and be prepared to remember it when you need to.

Physical Preparations

You will need a witness symbol for the pest. A witness symbol can be anything that is closely associated with the recipient of this spell. If it is a person, a photograph taken within the last few years is ideal. If there are other people in the photo, cut them out before proceeding. Alternatively, any small item that was once owned or handled by the person will also work. If none of these things are easily available to you, then a six-by-six inch square piece of parchment with the person's name written on it will do. Similar symbols will work for non-human pests. Such things as fur from a pesky animal, dirt from an ant hill, leaves from a virulent weed, or the pest's name on a piece of parchment are suitable.

Place the witness symbol in a small ceramic, metal, glass, or wooden container, and place the container on a stand located in the center of the area where you will cast your circle. The container must have a lid, but the lid must be off for the beginning of the ritual.

Ritual

Cast and cleanse your circle, and face east.

Proclaim your intention.

Ascend to your higher state. Face the direction in which you believe the pest to be located. If it is an ubiquitous type of pest, such as mice or fleas, then start by facing east and slowly turn clockwise. As you do, stay in touch with your sense of humor and read the following declaration:

> stray I pray
> go away, away
> go away and stay
> go the way
> of the émigré
> the castaway cast away
> the cast of a play
> on closing day
> the runaway run away
> the stray astray
> stay any delay
> leave today
> do as I say
> obey, obey

Hold the witness symbol in its container in front of you and, as you gaze at it, think of your pest. Continue to quietly think of the pest and of all of the past energy you have put into struggling with it.

Let the energy build. As you think of the energy you have expended on this pest, visualize this energy coming back to you. Visualize this energy entering you and building up in you. Be aware of any increase in tension and allow it to build. Remember any bad feelings you have had about this pest and allow that energy to build. Think of all of the energy that could continue to go into dealing with this pest if you do not rid yourself of it, and allow that to build. Allow any energy that is associated with this pest in any way whatsoever to come to you and to accumulate and to build in you. Continue to look at the witness symbol in its container. Let the energy build until you can contain it no longer.

Release the energy in one burst as you say the following words. Direct the energy toward the witness symbol. Just before you release the energy, remember the funniest part of the funniest thing that is connected with this old pest.

> *Energy is free*
> *Pest leave me*
> *So mote it be*

Place the lid on the container.

Descend from your higher state.

Disperse your circle.

Follow-up
Take the container with the witness symbol in it to a remote location far from your home (or wherever the pest was a problem) and hide it where there is no chance anyone else will find it. When your pest is gone, retrieve the container. Dispose of the witness symbol and wash the container. If you plan to use this container in another ritual, be sure to purify it again.

ACHIEVING A WILLED PURPOSE

(Or Success in a Pursuit)

This spell relies on the power of Will and the magical correspondences of two herbs. Unlike many of the spells in this book, it has more to do with changes you wish to make in the world, rather than changes within yourself. Examples might include such things as getting a job, being accepted at a university, or finding an apartment to rent. This is not to say that you may not need to make certain changes in order to have the magic work. The Self-Preparation section is designed to prepare the ground for any such changes that may be required.

Self-Preparation

Enter a light to medium trance. In your trance, imagine that you have already achieved your goal. Make this experience as real as you can. If you have any difficulty, invoke the Law of Pretending and act as if your goal is realized.

Once you have the sense that your goal is complete, write a brief statement of your goal or purpose on parchment (according to the instructions given in Physical Preparations below). Next, do a thorough review of just what you did in your visualization to achieve your purpose. Go over every step just as if it has really happened. It may help if you imagine that you are telling someone else how you did it, and you are instructing them on how to achieve the same goal. Continue this exercise until you are completely familiar with the necessary steps. When you are complete, come out of trance. Be prepared to act on what you learn from this exercise.

It is particularly important when working this spell that you have a clear, well-formed intention.

Physical Preparations

Cut a five-by-five inch piece of parchment for use in the Self-Preparation exercise. Once you have done the exercise, fold the parchment into thirds in one direction and then again into thirds in the other, so that it forms a small square slightly less than two inches on each side.

198

In addition to the folded parchment, you will need the following items: a bay leaf, powdered ginger, and a small cloth pouch or bag. The pouch can be made of any natural fabric other than silk, and should be just large enough to contain the folded parchment, the bay leaf, and ginger. Use only a small pinch of ginger, as too much ginger can offset the balance of the bay leaf. The ginger can be put on a small piece of parchment or in some special container. Place all of these materials on a stand in the center of the area where you will be casting your circle.

Ritual

Cast and cleanse your circle, and face east with the stand in front of you.

Proclaim your intention.

Ascend to your higher state.

Place the herbs and parchment in the pouch in the following order: the parchment, then the bay leaf, and lastly the ginger. As you place these items in the pouch, recite the following words:

> *This spell is from simple formulae*
> *of alchemy many times used*
> *of magic that works in the twinkle of an eye*
> *of sorcery that is never abused*

Hold the pouch in your right hand and this book in your left hand. Read the following words, speaking forcefully. You are making a pronouncement to the universe:

> **Magic of the east, I Will thee guide my intellect and thoughts and ideas in my pursuit to [state intention] so they remain in alignment with my higher self and true nature, and ally thyself to my purpose.**

Move clockwise, to the north side of the stand, and face south. Still holding the pouch and this book, read the following words:

Magic of the south, I Will thee draw out any courage I may need and direct any changes I must make in my pursuit to [state intention] so that they remain in concordance with my higher self and true nature, and ally thyself to my purpose.

Move clockwise to the east side of the stand, and face west. Still holding the pouch and this book, read the following words:

Magic of the west, I Will thee temper my emotions and hone my intuition in my pursuit to [name intention] so that they stay on course with my higher self and my true nature, and ally thyself to my purpose.

Move clockwise to the south side of the stand, and face north. Still holding the pouch and this book, read the following words:

Magic of the north, I Will thee instruct my body and inform my actions in my pursuit to [name intention] so that they are in accord with my higher self and my true nature, and ally thyself to my purpose.

Move clockwise to the west side of the stand, and again face east. Before you begin to move, set this book open on the stand. As you move, continue holding the pouch in your right hand and recite the following words with conviction and force:

To this purpose I shall prevail,
In this matter my Will be done,
As magic does my cause avail,
Without harming anyone.

Descend from your higher state.

Disperse your circle.

Follow-up
Keep the pouch with you or nearby until your purpose is realized. Be aware of your role in accomplishing your purpose, and take whatever action is required. Then LET GO and allow the magic to work.

HELPING ANOTHER PERSON
ACHIEVE A WILLED PURPOSE

Unlike any of the other spells in this book, this one is intended to be worked directly for the benefit of another person. Examples might include such things as helping a friend find an apartment to rent or improve their financial situation.

There are a variety of ways you can work a spell for another person. The other person can:

1. Be present in your circle during the Ritual after participating in the Self-Preparation stage.

2. Participate in the Self-Preparation stage but not be present during the Ritual.

3. Be aware you are casting a spell for them, but not participate in either the Self-Preparation or Ritual stages.

4. Not be aware you are casting a spell for them.

Your comfort level with another person present, the other person's comfort level and attitudes about magic, as well as time and distance constraints on you and the other person, will determine which of these situations is appropriate.

Situation 1 provides the easiest method to realize your intention. The level of difficulty increases from 2 through 4. There are a number of reasons for this. Situations 3 and 4 fail to provide the recipient of the spell with any formal preparation, the importance of which has been stressed throughout this volume. Because the other person is aware a spell is being cast for their benefit, situation 3 does, however, allow the other person's unconscious some level of informal, personal preparedness. Although situation 2 includes formal Self-Preparation, it deprives the recipient of the added experience of situation 1; that is, the powerful effect of being in the circle as magic is being worked.

Situation 4, in which the recipient is completely unaware that a spell is being cast, is by no means a condition for a spell to fail. In fact, it even has its own small set of advantages, including the fact that any conscious or unconscious resistance to magic on the part of the recipient will not interfere. This situation does, however, call for a very concentrated act of Will on the part of the person casting the spell. For this particular spell, it also means that the preparation and use of the specified herbs and other items is especially important.

Self-Preparation

The following instructions are divided into two parts: those for the recipient and those for you, the person working the spell. Obviously, the first part will be skipped if the recipient is not present for the Self-Preparation stage.

Recipient: Instruct the recipient to imagine that they have already realized their intention. Coach them to make this experience as real as they can, using all of their senses. If they have any difficulty, invoke the Law of Pretending and tell them to pretend they have met their goal.

Once the recipient has the sense of what it will be like when the intention is realized, have them write a brief statement of their goal or purpose on parchment (according to the instructions given in Physical Preparations below). Next, have the recipient thoroughly review what they did to achieve their purpose. Have them go over every step just as if it has really happened. One of the best ways to accomplish this is to interview the recipient, asking specific questions about how they managed each step in achieving the goal. If you feel that certain steps are being left out or glossed over in a cursory manner, ask them about it. Continue this exercise until you and the recipient are completely familiar with the necessary steps. When you are complete, instruct the recipient that they should be prepared to act on what they have learned from this exercise.

It is particularly important when working this spell that the recipient have a clear, well-formed intention. This may require some coaching on your part.

You: Be sure you have a clear image and statement for the intention of this spell. To the best of your ability, ensure that this intention matches that of the recipient's in every way. Review the short section in chapter 3 on Working Spells for Others, page 87.

Physical Preparations

Cut a 5 x 5 inch piece of parchment for use in the Self-Preparation exercise. Once you have done the exercise, fold the parchment into thirds in one direction and then again into thirds in the other, so that it forms a small square slightly less than 2 inches on each side.

In addition to the folded parchment, you will need the following items: a bay leaf, powdered ginger and a small cloth pouch or bag. The pouch can be made of any natural fabric other than silk and should be just large enough to contain the folded parchment, the bay leaf, and ginger. Use only a small pinch of ginger as too much ginger can offset the balance of the bay leaf. The ginger can be put on a small piece of parchment or in some special container. Place all of the materials on a stand in the center of the area where you will be casting your circle.

Ritual

Cast and cleanse your circle, and face east with the stand in front of you. If the recipient of this spell is present, have them stand inside the circle near the Eastern periphery for the duration of the ritual.

Proclaim your intention.

Ascend to your higher state.

Place the ingredients in the pouch in the following order: the parchment, then the bay leaf and lastly the ginger. As you place these in the pouch recite the following words:

This spell is from simple formulae
Of alchemy many times used
Of magic that works in the twinkle of an eye
Of sorcery that is never abused

Hold the pouch in your right hand and this book in your left hand. Read the following words. Speak forcefully. You are making an pronouncement to the universe:

Magic of the east, I Will thee guide [name of recipient]'s intellect and thoughts and ideas in [his or her] pursuit to [state intention] so they remain in alignment with [his or her] higher self and true nature, and ally thyself to [his or her] purpose.

Move clockwise to the north side of the stand and face south. Still holding the pouch in your right hand and this book in your left hand, read the following words:

Magic of the south, I Will thee draw out any courage [name of recipient] many need and direct any changes [he or she] must make in pursuit to [state intention] so that they remain in concordance with [his or her] higher self and true nature, and ally thyself to [his or her] purpose.

Move clockwise to the east side of the stand and face west. Still holding the pouch and this book, read the following words:

Magic of the west, I Will thee temper [name of recipient]'s emotions and hone [his or her] intuition in [his or her] pursuit to [name intention] so that they stay true to the course of [his or her] higher self and true nature, and ally thyself to [his or her] purpose.

Move clockwise to the south side of the stand and face north. Still holding the pouch and this book, read the following words:

Magic of the north, I Will thee instruct [name of recipient]'s body and inform [his or her] actions in [his or her] pursuit to [name intention] so that they are in accord with [his or her] higher self and true nature, and ally thyself to [his or her] purpose.

Move clockwise to the west side of the stand and face east. Before you begin to move, set this book open on the stand. As you move continue holding the pouch in your right hand and recite the following words with conviction and force:

To this purpose I shall prevail,
In this matter my Will be done,
As magic does this cause avail,
Without harming anyone.

Descend from your higher state.

Disperse your circle.

Follow-up

If the recipient is unaware that you have cast this spell, then place the pouch in close proximity to some object associated with them, such as a photograph or personal belonging.

If the recipient is aware of the spell, instruct them to carry the pouch with them or keep it nearby until their purpose is realized. Remind the recipient that they need to be aware of their role in realizing this intention and they should take whatever action is required. Other than this, instruct them to LET GO and allow the magic to work.

MAKING A DIFFICULT DECISION

Sometimes when you have an important decision to make, it seems like there is no way to know what is right. You can go over and over what you know about your choices—what the consequence of each might be, what is important to you and others, and what seems to be the right thing to do—and still arrive at an impasse. At such times, the old adage "All important decisions are made based on insufficient information" rings truer than ever. This aphorism turns out to be incomplete, however. It should read, "All important decisions are made based upon insufficient conscious information." The information exists somewhere, if not in your unconscious mind, then somewhere else in your universe. This is where magic comes in. This spell is the key to gaining access to the universe of information that is magically available to you. Once you possess this information, the right decision comes naturally and easily, even if you never consciously understand the reasons behind it.

Self-Preparation
Make a list of all of the choices you have regarding this decision. For example, perhaps you have been offered a better paying, more interesting job, but it would mean moving to a part of the country you do not care for. In such a situation, you may have only two conscious choices: take the job and move, or do not take the job and stay. Visualize, feel, and hear everything that you consciously know about each choice. It is important that you take a full inventory of the various possibilities, benefits, liabilities, consequences, and unknown factors that are associated with each choice. Make sure you keep each choice separate and distinct. Give each choice a name or title (for instance, you could call the choices "take the job" and "don't take the job"). Know that as you consciously do this exercise, your unconscious mind is doing the same thing in its own unique way.

Physical Preparations
You will need to collect several decision stones, one for each choice (stones of known choice), plus an additional one (the stone of hidden choice). For instance, in the example of the new job offer mentioned above, you would need three stones: two for

your conscious choices and an extra stone of hidden choice. Each stone should be at least an inch across but small enough to fit into the palm of your closed hand. Of equal importance, each stone should be distinctly different from the others in shape and texture. Take your time and take care when you choose the stones. Allow your intuition or aesthetic sense to come into play. For each choice, select a specific stone that feels just right for that option.

You will also need a cloth bag large enough to hold all of the stones, and with an opening big enough to allow you to reach inside. The bag can be made of any natural material, except silk. Place the stones and the bag on a stand in the center of the area where you plan to cast your circle. Be sure to purify these materials before using them in your ritual.

Ritual
Cast and cleanse your circle, and face east, with the stand in front of you.

Proclaim your intention.

Ascend to your higher state. Recite the following words:

> *This ritual to decide upon the best choice available to me regarding [state what you are deciding about] is well and truly begun.*

Pick up the first stone of known choice and read the following words, projecting your Will with forceful conviction:

> **This is the stone of [name the choice] and I Will it be infused with all knowledge of this choice and all consequences of this choice and all aspects of this choice and that nothing whatsoever about this choice remain concealed or absent from this stone.**

Feel the stone as you think of the choice. Just as you did in your preparation, visualize, feel, and hear everything that you consciously know about this choice (knowing that your unconscious mind is doing the same). As you are doing this, turn the stone over and over in your hand, paying close attention to its feel. Continue this process until you have completed your review of this choice and you are completely familiar with the feel of the stone. Be sure that you can recognize it apart from the other stones immediately upon picking it up.

Repeat this process for each stone of known choice, each time reading the following words and using the appropriate choice name:

> This is the stone of [name the choice] and I Will it be infused with all knowledge of this choice and all consequences of this choice and all aspects of this choice and that nothing whatsoever about this choice remain concealed or absent from this stone.

Pick up the stone of hidden choice last, after each of the stones of known choice has been infused with the knowledge of the choice it represents. Read the following words:

> This is the stone of hidden choice and I know not whether this choice be real or phantom and if real I know not whether this choice be worthy or corrupt and if worthy I know not whether it be best or not and if best I know not what its nature be. If this choice be real, I Will that this stone be infused with all knowledge of this choice and all consequences of this choice and all aspects of this choice and that nothing whatsoever about this choice remain concealed or absent from this stone and that should this choice reveal itself as best, that it reveal itself in full and make its nature and appearance known in all particulars. And if this choice be phantom, I Will that this fine stone remain silent and inert as is true to its nature as a stone and that it not participate in the matters pertaining to my decision.

Place all of the stones in the cloth bag. Close your eyes, reach your hand into the bag, and mix the stones around. Set the bag down in front of you. Keeping your eyes closed, recite the following words from memory:

> *Wisdom of Chokmah*
> *Knowing in me*
> *Understanding of Binah**
> *I call for all three*

---

* See footnote 6, following page.

Emanations
Radiations
Flowing to me
Flowing through me
Into eyes that feel
Into hands that see

Visualize wisdom and understanding flowing into you as a stream of warm, white light coming from above. With your eyes closed, relax into your quiet, totally receptive state. Visualize the stream of light entering the top of your head. Imagine two other streams of light—those of your inner knowing—emanating from your heart and from your mind. Imagine that all three streams are converging inside you, running down your right arm and out your extended index finger.

With eyes closed, look down at the imagined cloth bag in front of you. In your mind's eye, see it just as you would if your physical eyes were open. Point your right index finger toward the bag and visualize the converging streams of wisdom's light infusing the bag. Hold the gaze of your mind's eye on the bag, watching it change color as the light permeates it. See it first change to red, and then gradually progress through the colors of the spectrum—orange, yellow, green, blue, and finally purple. The bag will become purple when it is saturated with wisdom's light. At the point of saturation, visualize the stream of light quickly dissipating, and finally disappearing.

In your imagination, choose a stone. Visualize that you reach into the bag with your right hand and grab the first stone you find. Do not remove it from the imaginary bag. Rather, turn it over and over in your hand until you recognize it. This is the stone of your best choice. With your eyes still closed, release this stone inside the bag and allow the bag to change from purple back to its original color.

Open your eyes and return to your physical body. Proceed depending on what stone you picked in your visualization. If you picked a stone of known choice, which is

---

6. Chokmah and Binah are two points on the Tree of Life (also refered to as the Ten Sefiroth) of the Qabala; they represent the essence of wisdom and understanding, respectively.

most often the case, then your path and decision are clear. Proceed directly with dispersing your circle.

Only if you picked the stone of hidden choice, read the words:

> The Wisdom and Understanding of Chokmah and Binah is perfect.
> I am an earthly manifestation of these emanations.
> I draw upon all the Wisdom and Understanding I need.
> I draw upon my ability to live in perfect truth.
> I Will that the nature and particulars of this choice be revealed to me.
> I remain receptive to this revelation for the next [state a time].

Intuitively choose a time period as you are reciting the very last line. Refrain from consciously rehearsing or determining a time period beforehand. Accept whatever time period comes spontaneously out of your mouth. This could be hours or days, but it is generally not less than one hour, nor longer than about two weeks.

Descend from your higher state.

Disperse your circle.

Follow-up

If you picked the stone of hidden choice, keep the stone with you or near you at all times and be sure to touch it from time to time. Put the bag with the remaining stones away in a safe place. During the period that follows, be alert to anything that reveals the hidden choice. This could be in the form of random thoughts, casual words spoken by friends, or something you hear on the radio or read in the newspaper or a book. It could manifest as the slow formation of another choice in your mind, or the sudden realization about the best decision. Remember that magic often produces results from unexpected sources. Be receptive and alert to everything around you.

If nothing has revealed itself at the end of the chosen time period, it is an indication that considering the hidden choice has shifted something making one of the other choices best. In this event, return the stone of hidden choice to the location where you found it, and repeat this ritual again.

HELPING YOUR DISTRESSED PLANT OR ANIMAL

When working this spell, you will act as a conduit for healing energy. The witness object and other substances you use in the spell provide the magical correspondences and associations required to store, direct, and release that energy to your purpose.

Self-Preparation

Determine which of your hands is your receiving hand and which is your giving hand. For right-handed people, the giving hand is usually the right and the receiving hand is usually the left. For left-handed people, the opposite usually holds true. To test this in yourself, imagine the following: There is a stream of white energy flowing past you. You are a perfect conduit for this energy and you can direct it anywhere by allowing it to enter one of your hands, flow through your arm and body, and exit through the other arm and hand. In your mind, try this with the stream flowing both ways. First, visualize it going in your left hand and out your right hand, and then the other way around. Which one feels more natural? If you cannot experience any difference, then assume you fit the usual pattern based upon your handedness.

Once again, visualize the energy flowing into your receiving hand and out your giving hand, allowing the energy to flow freely through you. This requires no work on your part. The energy neither adds anything to you, nor takes anything from you. You are purely a magical conduit. This exercise of imagining energy flowing through you, and being directed by you, is similar to what you will be doing during the ritual.

Physical Preparations

You will need the following items: a clove of garlic, a small green stone, a sage leaf (or two or three pinches of dried or powdered sage), a small cloth pouch or bag, and a witness object. If pain is involved, a horse chestnut is also useful, but not necessary.

If dried or powdered sage is used, place several pinches in a small dish or other special container (or on a piece of parchment). The pouch can be made of any natural fabric other than silk, and should be just large enough to contain all of the other items. The witness object can be anything closely associated with the plant or animal; for example, a snippet of fur, a leaf, a pinch of dirt from the base of the plant, or a photo of the plant or animal.

Place all of the items on a stand located in the center of the area where you will cast your circle.

Ritual

Cast and cleanse your circle, and face east.

Proclaim your intention.

Ascend to your higher state.

Place each object in the pouch in the following order: sage, garlic, stone, witness object, and horse chestnut, if used. As you place each item in the pouch, recite the following words:

> *Sage, clear mind*
> *Garlic, health to find*
> *Stone, remove distress*
> *Object to witness*
> *[Horse nut, pain be less]*

Set the pouch on the stand after all of the objects have been placed in it, and read the following words:

> I Will the healing energy which comes from the one source of all energy and power and love, of which I am a perfect manifestation, flow through me and to be directed to this living being [name of animal or plant] which is under my custodianship and which relies on me and which at this moment is much possessed of woe and disquietude.

Receive and direct the flow of healing energy. Raise your receiving hand, palm up in front of you, over the level of your head. Hold your giving hand over the pouch, with your palm down. Imagine warm, white healing light streaming down from overhead, into your receiving hand, and out your giving hand. Visualize your plant or animal as present in the circle. Visualize the pouch receiving the energy flow. As it absorbs more and more healing energy, see it glow increasingly brighter as the energy builds. Recite the following words as you see the energy accumulating in the pouch. Repeat the words over and over again, increasing the tempo and volume of your voice each time.

> *Energy flow*
> *To below*
> *From above*
> *Through love*
> *Through me*
> *To thee [name of plant or animal]*

Release the energy. When the tension reaches a peak and the pouch is completely saturated, stop suddenly. Pause for a very brief moment, and then, in a quiet but firm voice, say the words:

> *I Will good healing be done*
> *With harm to come to none*

Visualize the stream of light dissipating and finally disappearing.

Descend from your higher state.

Disperse your circle.

Follow-up

Place the pouch near the plant or near a place where the animal spends much time. In the following hours and days, imagine that the healing energy absorbed into the pouch is radiating out to the troubled being. Also be attentive to any thoughts or ideas that occur to you, or any information that comes to you regarding specific things you may do to help, or ways in which you can attend to the plant or animal. Otherwise, LET GO and allow the magic to work.

BRINGING OUT THE SUN

This is a simple, basic ritual that uses the principle of building a strong reserve of psychic energy and then releasing it in one sudden burst of Will.

Self-Preparation

Take a look outside and carefully observe the sky. Hold this image in your mind. Center yourself and take a few minutes to visualize the clouds beginning to disperse. Continue to visualize until the sun bursts through in your imagination. Persevere until you can visualize every cloud is gone and there are completely clear skies above.

Physical Preparations

Place a stand in the center of the location where you plan to cast your circle.

Ritual

This ritual is best cast during daylight hours.

Cast and cleanse your circle, and face east.

Proclaim your intention.

Ascend to your higher state. Repeat the mental imagery exercise you practiced in the Self-Preparation stage. In your mind, watch the sky slowly change from its present state to clear skies. As you do this, feel the difference in the atmosphere as the weather dramatically improves. Imagine that you are outside and can feel the warmth of the sun on your face.

Chant repeatedly once you can feel the warmth. Start with a firm voice, but with a low volume and slow tempo. Build both the volume and tempo as you continue to repeat the following words. Feel the tension and the energy build as you continue to chant. If you have been experiencing cloud cover without rain, then leave out the first verse and start with the word CLOUD.

Rain
Drain
Dryn
Dry

To the rain
I say goodbye

Cloud
Clour
Cloar
Clear
I Will the
Clouds to disappear

Gone
Sone
Son
Sun

See how easily
it is done

Build toward a climax. Once the build-up of tension starts to become uncomfortable, repeat the words to the chant two or three more times.

Release the psychic energy. Speak the following words with maximum force and volume. As you do, feel the force of your Will travel out on the tremendous stream of your psychic energy.

I Will it done
For the goodness of all
With harm to none

Descend from your higher state.

Disperse your circle. LET GO and allow the magic to work.

BRINGING THE RAIN

This spell combines the power of Will with the principle of sympathetic magic. This is a very simple ritual. For those who enjoy a light-hearted mood and the occasional glass of champagne, it is also a pleasant one. Be very clear in your intention to specify the amount of rain and in what form you want it. You would not want to be responsible for a local monsoon.

Self-Preparation

Take a look outside and carefully observe the sky. Now sit quietly, and in your imagination, see, hear, and feel the conditions for rain starting to build. Most people have a very good idea of what this is like in their area. The weather most frequently comes from one general direction and the clouds form in a particular way. There is a change in the smell of the air and the feel of the atmosphere. At some point, the wind may pick up, slow down, or shift in direction. There are sounds associated with an approaching rain system, and the colors in the landscape start to transform. Continue with this exercise and slowly build to an imaginary rain shower.

Physical Preparations

Place a chair and a stand in the center of the location where you plan to cast your circle. Place a champagne glass, towel, and a bottle of respectable champagne or other quality sparkling wine on the stand. If you do not drink alcoholic beverages under any circumstances, then a bottle of nonalcoholic sparkling wine can be used.

Ritual

Cast and cleanse your circle, and face east.

Proclaim your intention.

Ascend to your higher state. Face the direction from which most of your weather comes. If you are not sure of this, then face west, as this is a good bet in much of the world.

Bring on a rainstorm. Sit quietly, sustain a light and cheerful mood, and take some time to let your imagination see the sky change from its present appearance to increasingly covered in rain clouds. Visualize the clouds becoming darker and denser, and feel the air grow heavier with humidity. With your mind's ear, listen to the increasing stillness as a rain storm approaches. Notice the elevation in atmospheric and psychic energy that precedes a strong rain, and remind yourself how helpful such an energy build-up can be in working strong magic. Maintain your good mood throughout the building of your imagination's storm. When you can maximally feel the imminent presence of the rainstorm, but before the rain actually comes, read the following words with good cheer.

> **Rain, Rain you needn't remain,**
> **Mainly on the plains of Spain,**
> **Abstain from obeying this old refrain;**
> **Sustain a campaign to increase your domain;**
> **Come pour your blessings on this terrain,**
> **For 'tis you that I praise,**
> **As my glass I raise,**
> **To toast you with stormy champagne.**

Carefully open the champagne bottle over the towel so as not to spill any within the sanctity of your circle. Pour some champagne into your glass. Consciously observe as it pours and be aware of its inherent nature (a mixture of gas and liquid) and its correspondence to rain (water vapor and liquid water). Take a small sip, hold the glass up in a toast, and say the following words. As you do, release any tension that has built up since conjuring your imaginary rainstorm. Visualize and feel the rain finally coming.

> *I Will thee Rain come anon*
> *With harm to none hereupon*

Descend from your higher state.

Disperse your circle. LET GO and allow the magic to work.

Follow-up

Share the rest of the champagne with friends. Enjoy yourself and talk about anything but the rain.

STOPPING SOMEONE
WHO TALKS TOO MUCH

Will to a purpose, seasoned with a bit of mischievousness and humor, works wonders in this spell to slow someone down who normally insists on talking too much.

Self-Preparation

Take a few minutes to visualize this person in some absurd or humorous condition. Being naked, except for rubber gloves and sneakers, or having changed from male to female (or the other way around), or being followed by a loyal band of green squirrels are possible examples. You should feel both enjoyment and amusement as you visualize your image. When you have the image that you want, imprint it on your mind.

Physical Preparations

You will cleanse your circle with lemon water rather than with the usual rosemary tea. Prepare the water several days before you plan to cast your spell. Squeeze the juice from ⅛ of a lemon (about a normal wedge) into a cup of water, and place it in the refrigerator. Clean the lemon pulp from the peel of the lemon wedge and dry the peel. This can be done by setting it on a radiator or heat grate, or in the sun for several days.

Place the dried peel and the cleansing vessel containing the lemon water on the stand located in the center of the area where you will be casting your circle.

Ritual

Cast and cleanse your circle, and face east. Use the lemon water to cleanse your circle in the same manner that you would normally use rosemary tea.

Proclaim your intention.

Ascend to your higher state. Face the direction where you believe the fast talker is located. If you are not sure of the person's whereabouts at the time of casting your spell, then face the direction of their home or workplace. If none of this information is available to you, then use your intuition as to what direction to face.

Remember the absurd mental image that you created during the Self-Preparation exercise. As the image and the associated feelings of amusement come back to you, hold the lemon peel up to your nose and smell it. Repeat this three times, that is, visualizing the image while smelling the lemon peel. When you have done this, place the lemon peel back on the stand. Read the following words while attempting to stay in touch with the feelings from your image. Follow the visual cues and let your voice trail off and eventually become stilled.

I Will that your ceaseless utterances and streams of verbose vapidity,
are reduced each passing minute to ease the verbal stupidity,
as your words spew forth with astounding fecundity,
about the banal and inane with such rapidity,
that either one's head spins nauseously,
or one seeks most desperately,
to escape from the reality,
of hearing incessantly,
and relentlessly,
talking,
talk,
SH
SH
SH
SH
SH
SH
SH
Sh
Sh
Sh
sh
sh
sh
sh
sh
sh
sh

Descend from your higher state.

Disperse your circle.

Follow-up

Have the lemon peel with you the next time you are in the company of this person. Covertly take out the peel and smell it periodically while you are with them. You may be surprised by what has changed in them and in you.

APPENDICES

ACHIEVING
ALTERED STATES:
A SUMMARY OUTLINE

Steps to Self-Hypnosis

Step 1. Relax Your Entire Body. Assume a favored position and, starting with your toes, progressively relax each part of your body right up to the top of your head.

Step 2. Travel Down. Enter the gateway by saying the words, "Now I enter the gateway to my inner self." In your imagination, visualize that you are in a very comfortable psychic elevator (or bubble or platform) and start slowly down from the top floor to lower floors. Visualize a sign with the following words and, in your mind, recite them from memory:

> *The deeper you go, the more relaxed and comfortable and alert you become and the more capable you become of learning new things in new ways.*

Remind yourself that with each lower floor you are slowly going deeper into trance.

Step 3. Perform a Task. When you have arrived at a level of trance that suits you, visualize stopping your psychic elevator. From this state, make any suggestions to yourself that you consider beneficial, or perform whatever mental or emotional tasks are called for in working a specific spell.

Step 4. Return from Trance. When you are ready to come up out of trance, in your imagination, push the "up" button and start ascending in your psychic elevator. In your mind, hear the following words as if they are coming from a recorded message over the elevator's public address system:

As you ascend, you will find yourself more and more refreshed and alert with every floor you pass. When you reach the top you will be fully refreshed and alert.

When you reach the top, you will be completely out of trance. Open your eyes.

Streamlining

As you become more proficient in entering into a self-induced trance, you can begin to streamline the process by gradually eliminating the visualization of the elevator and relying solely on entering the gateway as a means of quickly going through all of the steps into whatever level of trance suits you.

Ascending to a Higher State

Step 1. Enter into Trance. Enter a medium trance by starting at the top floor as usual and descending to the fourth or fifth floor level.

Step 2. Enter the Gateway to your Higher State. Say the words, "Now the gateway to my higher self opens," and visualize the gate opening.

Step 3. Ascend. Start the slow ascent up, but instead of stopping and leaving trance as you have in the past, continue on up past the top floor. Be conscious that you are moving up and beyond the place where you began.

Step 4. Break Through and Experience your Higher State. Visualize that you break through into a completely different realm. Stop your ascent here and open your eyes (if they are not already open). It is here that you can fully realize your higher self, your true nature.

Step 5. Descend from your Higher State. When you are ready to descend from your higher state, use your elevator to return down from your starting point at the top floor.

Streamlining

As you become proficient at ascending to your higher state, you can eliminate the need to first descend into trance. You can enter your higher state directly by simply entering the gateway to your higher state.

DESIGNING A WELL-FORMED INTENTION: A SUMMARY OUTLINE

Choose the Right Intention

This is the most basic criterion for a well-formed intention. Will realization of a particular intention improve your life or resolve your problems in the way you desire?

Be Free of Reservations and Doubts

You must want and approve of your intention 100 percent in body, mind, and spirit. Never ignore your doubts; they are signals that something needs to be changed.

Keep It Possible

Remember to limit your intentions to those things that the laws of nature permit.

Keep It Probable

The forces that must be put into play for the realization of a highly improbable intention are enormous. This can require very strong magic indeed, and can be beyond the limit of your range of abilities.

Size the Task Appropriately

Achieve big goals in a series of smaller steps.

Be Precise

The particulars should be spelled out as clearly and completely as is feasible.

Be Literal

Be sure you can state your intention in plain, simple language, free of metaphor, simile, and organ language.

State It Positively

It is preferable to state your intentions in positive statements, avoiding negating words like "not."

Identify the Essence

When intending complex or systemic changes, an alternative strategy is to accurately state the essence of what you want.

Get in Touch with How It Would Feel

If you can get in touch with what it would feel like to realize your intention, you have identified a very basic component of the essence of your intention.

Create Accurate Images

It is essential to have clear images or a series of images of what things would look like once your intention has been realized.

Write It Down

When you have completed forming a statement of your intention, write it down.

THE STEPS IN CASTING A SPELL: A SUMMARY OUTLINE

Designing a Well-Formed Intention

This topic is covered in detail in chapter 3, pages 64–71, and summarized in outline form in Appendix 2.

Rehearsal

Learn the ritual procedures for the specific spell you are working:

- Memorize the appropriate spoken words.

- Familiarize yourself with words that are to be read out loud.

Self-Preparation

Follow the Self-Preparation instructions for the specific spell you are working.

Physical Preparations

Purify items or substances to be used in the ritual, unless they are items (such as this book) that are used exclusively for working magic and have already been purified.

Follow the Physical Preparations instructions for the specific spell you are working.

Change into the clothing and jewelry you use when working magic.

Ritual

Centering Yourself

Compose yourself as described in the short process on page 76.

Casting a Magic Circle

Begin by facing East and slowly turn clockwise with your arm extended and your index finger pointing outward. Envisage an energy stream marking out the perimeter of a circle with you at the center. As you are casting your circle say the following:

Let this circle mark the boundary between the magical and the mundane, and within its perimeter let there be true sanctuary, where nothing may enter except that I Will it so.

Cleansing Your Circle

Unless otherwise stated in the instructions, rosemary tea is used (page 78) for cleansing.

Hold the tea vessel in your left hand. Facing East, dip the fingers of your right hand in the tea, and with a flicking motion, sprinkle water toward the East three times. As you do, say the words:

With the power of this herb of the Sun and the purity of this water, I cleanse the Eastern domain.

Turn clockwise and repeat this procedure, facing each of the remaining cardinal directions (saying the name of the appropriate direction each time).

Proclaiming Your Intention

Speak the following words:

> **This ritual is well and truly commenced to accomplish the purpose of my Will, which I proclaim to be as follows . . .**

Having memorized the final written version of your intention, state it fully in a firm, clear voice.

Casting Your Spell

Depending on the instructions for the particular spell you are working, you will either ascend to a higher state (page 59 and Appendix 1) or enter a trance (page 52 and Appendix 1).

Follow the procedures that you have memorized during the rehearsal phase. Use the headings in this book to cue you when necessary.

When reading from this book, hold the book open in one hand, leaving the other hand free. Passages to be recited from memory are printed in boldface type.

Dispersing Your Circle

Face East, and this time use your left hand to erase the circle. Slowly turn counterclockwise, allowing the energy of the circle to be reabsorbed into you. As you do this, say the words:

> **My work here is well and truly completed, and the circle is opened and dispersed until further needed.**

Visualize the circle disappearing and the boundaries of the magical space fading, until you have eradicated the entire circle.

Follow-up

Some spells require certain procedures to be followed after you have completed the ritual. Follow the instructions conscientiously.

THE PRACTICE SPELL
OF CHAPTER 3

A Practice Spell in the Format of Part II

This exercise is intended to familiarize you with the procedures of casting a spell and the experience of being in magical space. Once you are set up, it should take no more than about fifteen or twenty minutes. Practice it once a day for three or four days in row.

Self-Preparation

For a few minutes, invoke the Law of Pretending. Pretend that you are skilled and experienced at casting spells, and that you have been practicing magic for many years. You are about to cast this practice spell in an attempt to reexperience what it was like when you first started to practice magic.

Physical Preparations

An incense for stimulating your psychic and mental abilities is used in this spell. To make the incense, you will need a teaspoon of ground mace and a teaspoon of dried rosemary. Mix the two ingredients together and wrap this incense in a piece of parchment, or put it in a small covered container (made of any material but plastic). Keep this for use during the ritual. An incense holder and incense charcoal are also necessary.

These are available in occult shops, religious supply stores, and sometimes import stores that carry a large selection of brass items from India. Instructions for mixing and burning incense and for making your own incense burner can be found in Appendix 5. A yellow candle is needed to ignite the charcoal.

Place the incense holder, charcoal, incense, and a lighted yellow candle on a stand in the center of the area where you plan to cast your circle.[1,2]

Ritual[3]

Cast and cleanse your circle, and face East.

Proclaim your intention.[4]

Ascend to your higher state.

Light the incense charcoal with the yellow candle and place two pinches of the incense on it. The smoky vapors of both herbs stimulate psychic and mental awareness. Be aware of their essence as you proceed.

See the interior of the circle. Can you see the boundary of the space the circle defines? What does it look like? What do the objects and surfaces within the circle look like? What do you see with your eyes and what do you see with your imagination? As you spend more time in this magical space, these two ways of seeing will begin to merge, but only while in the circle.

---

1. Designing a well-formed intention and rehearsal are standard procedures that do not require specific instructions for each spell. They have therefore been omitted from the instructions in Part II.

2. The following procedures are part of the Physical Preparations of every spell, and therefore are omitted from the instructions in Part II: ensuring all items and substances to be used are purified, changing into the clothes and jewelry you reserve for working magic, and placing *Foundations of Magic* and the vessel of cleansing tea on the stand.

3. Centering yourself just before you begin the ritual is standard practice, and therefore omitted from the ritual instructions in Part II.

4. Normally you must form your own intention and memorize the wording of it prior to casting a spell. Since this practice spell is part of a learning exercise, the intention was specified for you. It is "to experience magical space and to learn about the magic within this circle, which I have cast and to claim its sanctuary as mine."

Feel the interior of the circle. What does it feel like to be in the circle? Do you sense the protection and the sanctity offered by the circle? What does the air feel like? How does your body feel? How is your mind?

Listen inside the circle. Notice the quality that silence has in the circle. Say something out loud and notice the sound of your own voice. Gently splash the cleansing tea with your fingers and listen to the sound it makes.

Attend to things outside the circle. As viewed from inside your circle, how do objects outside the circle look different from those inside of it? What is the quality of that difference? What do you notice about the sounds that emanate from outside the circle? Remind yourself that all everyday concerns lie outside the circle. Briefly think of one. Notice how its power to affect you is absent or greatly diminished.

Direct your Will. Forcefully speak the following proclamation from memory. As you speak, be aware of your Will being directed out beyond the boundaries of the circle, out to every corner of the universe to effect your purpose. Also be aware of your Will simultaneously being directed inward to every part of yourself, for you are the microcosm that corresponds to the macrocosm that is the universe.

> *Let my awareness, appreciation, and effective use of magical space increase boldly and rapidly and for the good of all. I Will it so with harm to come to none.*

Descend from your higher state.

Disperse your circle.

Follow-up

A few hours after you have dispersed your circle, reflect on the experience of having performed this ritual. For most people, the shift in perception that occurs inside the magic circle is immediate. For others, there is no apparent difference, at least in the beginning. This disparity in initial response is not an indicator of later proficiency. Everyone's awareness increases with practice, and each person comes to each new realization about magical space in their own time. Know that you are doing well.

HOW TO MAKE AN INCENSE BURNER

Stick or cone incense are not used in the rituals of *Foundations of Magic*. Rather, the various incenses that are called for are made from herbs or other common plants and benzoin gum. Burning this type of incense requires the use of an incense charcoal and an incense burner designed for use with the charcoal. The charcoals are cylindrical discs about 1 inch in diameter and ½-inch thick. They are chemically treated, so that they readily ignite if a flame is touched to their surface. To burn incense, simply light the charcoal and, when the starting chemical has burned off, place a few pinches of the incense on top of it. While the charcoal remains hot, you can continue to add incense as needed. The charcoals and incense burners can be purchased at occult or religious supply stores, either directly or through mail order. The burners can sometimes be found in import shops that carry a selection of Indian brass items. Alternatively, you can fashion your own incense burner as follows:

The basic component of the burner is an open metal or ceramic vessel 3 to 5 inches in diameter and deep enough to allow you to cover the bottom with at least 1 inch of dry sand or salt. A shallow bowl, deep-sided dish or ashtray is ideal. For the most basic incense holder, simply place 1 inch of sand or salt in the vessel, and put the charcoal in the center.

You can elaborate on this design by making a swinging incense holder, such as is recommended for the spell Attracting Money, Long-Term (page 138). You will need 3 lengths of lightweight, decorative chain, each are 12 to 18 inches long. The chain should be the type that allows you to open and reclose the links using pliers. Three holes, evenly spaced around the perimeter, must be drilled in the vessel to accommodate attaching the lengths of chain. Metal vessels are better suited to this as it is easier to drill holes in metal than in ceramic. An alternative to drilling holes is to locate a brass ashtray that already has filigreed openings around its perimeter. Attach the top link of each length of chain to a connecting ring. A keychain ring, finger ring, or metal drapery ring can be used for this purpose.

The herbs and spices that are used for incense in *Foundations of Magic* can be found in the spice section of most grocery stores. They are also available at health food stores and herb shops, as is benzoin gum. Traditionally, the herb or plant material that is used for incense is ground in a mortar with a pestle. In most cases, this is unnecessary, as most herbs and spices can be purchased in ground or powdered form. When fresh plant material is used, it is best dried (in the sun, oven, food dehydrator, or on a heat register) and finely crumbled between your fingers.

A word of caution: The charcoal burns quite hot, so take care that is it does not come into contact with combustible materials. Make sure to use enough sand or salt in the burner to insulate the bottom of it from excessive heat.

Appendix 6

MAKING A TALISMAN USING MAGIC SQUARES

A magic square is a table of consecutive numbers arranged such that the sum of any row, column, or diagonal is the same. For instance, in the magic square below the sum in every direction is 111 (you are invited to verify this for yourself). This is a six-by-six magic square, as there are six rows and six columns. There are also magic squares of other dimensions such as three-by-three or ten-by-ten.

Magic squares have intrigued people for thousands of years because of their mathematical and magical properties. The magical property that interests us here is the correspondence of certain squares to specific heavenly bodies, each corresponding to particular influences and magical attributes. Each of the seven planets of antiquity (the five planets visible with the naked eye plus the sun and the moon) has a specific magic square associated with it. When making a talisman, a planetary magic square is chosen based upon the purpose of the magic to be worked. For example, the following six-by-six magic square corresponds to the sun.

The correspondences between magic squares, planets, and colors (as well as many other correspondences) are listed in innumerable books, for those who wish to pursue the subject. The only talismans required to work the magic in *Foundations of Magic* are solar talismans used in Attracting the Right Love Partner, and therefore only the Magic Square of the Sun has been presented here.

6	32	3	34	35	1
7	11	27	28	8	30
19	14	16	15	23	24
18	20	22	21	17	13
25	29	10	9	26	12
36	5	33	4	2	31

Magic Square of the Sun

The system of making talismans using magic squares is based on Qabalistic traditions. Essential to this system is a special characteristic of the Hebrew alphabet in which each letter also represents a number. This correspondence of letters to numbers has been transposed to the English alphabet and is displayed in the following table.

1	2	3	4	5	6	7	8	9
A	B	C	D	E	F	G	H	I
J	K	L	M	N	O	P	Q	R
S	T	U	V	W	X	Y	Z	

Correspondence of Letters to Numbers

The following example demonstrates how to make a solar talisman for the name William. To begin, you will need a pencil or pen and a Magic Square of the Sun. The square should be about the same size as the one on this page, no larger. Start on the number 5, which corresponds to W, the first letter in William. On the magic square, draw a line from 5 to 9 (9 corresponds to I, the second letter in the name). Continue this procedure of drawing lines between the numbers that correspond to the consecutive letters in the name. When you are through, you should have a zigzag line like the one below. This line is referred to as a solar sigil of William. Notice that when a line doubles back on itself, as occurs when the 1–4 line doubles back on the 9–1 line, the line changes direction with a curve rather than a sharp angle. Notice also that the double letter L in the name is denoted by a double loop at its corresponding number 3. It is conventional to begin the line with a very small circle and end it with a small T.

6	32	3	34	35	1
7	11	27	28	8	30
19	14	16	15	23	24
18	20	22	21	17	13
25	29	10	9	26	12
36	5	33	4	2	31

Magic Square of the Sun
with the Sigil of William

The next step is to draw the sigil (without the magic square) onto a paper circle 2 to 3 inches in diameter. Because this is a solar sigil, it should be drawn onto yellow paper, using either gold or white ink. If the yellow paper is thin and translucent enough, you can trace the sigil directly. If the paper is opaque, you can lay your drawing of the sigil on top of the paper circle in the magic square and, using heavy pressure, trace the sigil with a ballpoint pen. This will leave an impression on the paper circle that you can trace with ink. An example of a completed talisman is shown as follows.

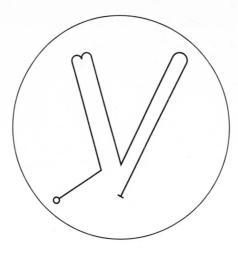

Talisman with the Solar Sigil for William

INDEX

almonds, 145–147
artificial memory, 46–47
astral body, 20, 120–121, 132–133, 185–187
astral plane, 20, 120, 132, 185
astral travel (projection), 20, 133

basil, 25, 72, 139
bay leaf, 199, 203
belief (in magic), 3, 15
benzoin, 139, 145, 240

centering yourself, 46, 75–78, 82, 89
champagne, 216–218
cinnamon, 145
clothes and jewelry used in ritual, 73–74
conscious mind, defined, 32–33
conscious mind and incubation, 50
correspondences, 25, 198, 211
Crowley, Aleister, 11–12, 15

decision stones, 206, 208
Dee, John, 15
deosil, 77

Emerald Tablet, 24, 180
Enochian magic, 15
Erickson, Milton, 28
ethics of casting spells, 63, 87–88

feelings and intentions, 70
feelings and memory, 43–44, 47, 169–170,
    188–189

garlic, 211–212
gateway to higher state, 54–55, 57–61
gateway to trance, 54, 59
ginger, 145–147, 199, 203
Golden Dawn, Hermetic Order of the, 5, 15

Hebrew, 19
herbs, 23, 25, 79, 81–82, 103, 139, 145, 149,
    179–180, 198–199, 202
Hermes Trismegistus, 24, 179–181
Hermetic magic, 11, 15, 179
High John the Conqueror root, 148–149
higher self, 14, 20–21, 24, 59–60, 199–200,
    204
higher self, defined, 20–21

higher state, 21, 59–61, 79, 82–83, 93–94, 99, 101, 103–104, 107–108, 111, 113, 119, 121, 125, 135, 137, 141–142, 146–147, 149–150, 153, 156–157, 159, 161, 163–165, 167–168, 176, 178, 181, 184, 187, 193–194, 196–197, 199–200, 203, 205, 207, 210, 212–217, 219, 221

horse chestnut, 119, 121, 123–124, 211–212

humor, 51–52, 166, 181, 195–196, 219

hypnotic trance, defined, 52, 54

hypnotic trance, steps to self hypnosis, 52, 54

images, mental, and memory, 43
  and thoughts, 38, 129, 141
  in forming intentions, 47–51
  out of awareness, 39

incense, 81–82, 138–141, 145–146, 179–180

incubation, 47–48, 50

intention, 12, 24–25, 32, 34–37, 47–51, 63–71, 73, 79–82, 85–86, 88, 93, 98–99, 103, 106–107, 110–111, 115, 119, 123, 128–129, 132, 135–136, 140, 146, 149, 153, 157, 160–161, 164, 167, 171, 176, 180, 184, 190, 192–193, 196, 198–205, 207, 212, 214, 216, 219
  designing, 47, 63–64, 81, 88, 184
  proclaiming, 79
  and incubation, 47

Isis, 19

Law of Association, First, 24–25

Law of Association, Second, 24

Law of Correspondences, 25

Law of Levels, 24

Law of Pretending, 17, 28, 31, 39, 43–44, 58, 70, 80–81, 98, 106, 128, 169, 175, 188, 198, 202
  explained, 28–31

Law of Prudence, 23, 25, 89, 182

Law of Will, 24

lemon(s), 219–220, 222

letting go, 23, 35, 47, 50, 94, 101, 105, 113, 117, 121, 130, 133, 137, 142, 156, 159, 163, 165, 168, 173, 191, 200, 205, 213, 215, 217

mace, 81–82

magic, defined, 11–16
  high and low, 14
  old and new, 13, 18, 84
  white and black, 13–14, 87, 148
  and power, 14–15, 18–19, 156, 159, 162, 190–191, 216
  and religion, 15
  and science, 12, 15

magic circle, casting, 21, 72, 76–78, 80, 82–83, 98, 111, 140, 153, 157, 179–180, 199, 203, 219
  cleansing, 78–79
  dispersing, 77, 80, 83, 210
  permanent, 77

magic squares, 241–243

magical time and space, 18, 21, 74–76, 78, 80–84, 122–123

marbles, 103

Mars, 25

memories, 8, 31, 42–47, 71, 82, 115–117, 121, 125, 131, 140, 149, 152–153, 157, 169–173, 175–177, 183, 188–191, 208

mercury and incubation, 139

metaphors, 19, 27, 33, 67–68, 71, 126, 129–130, 192

mirror, 40, 72, 74, 115–117, 166, 168, 174–177

nutmeg, 139–141

observer, 8, 42–43, 45, 93–94, 114, 116, 118, 132, 154, 192
olive oil, 139–141
organ language, 68
Osiris, 19

participant, 8, 42–45, 47, 94, 114, 116, 118, 131–132, 186, 192
pentagram(s), 160, 162
physical preparation, 72, 179
power over, 13–15, 30, 157
power through, 14–15, 30, 157
practice spell, 81–82, 89
problems, benefits from, 33–34, 36, 160
    and difficulties, 3, 8, 17, 22, 32–37, 39, 43, 47–49, 51, 53–55, 58, 64–65, 68, 80, 86, 98, 106, 110, 123, 143, 160–161, 163, 166–167, 169, 188, 195, 197–198, 201–202
purification of articles and elements, 72–73, 78

Qabala, 5, 11, 15, 209
quantum mechanics, 66

rehearsal, 7, 29, 63, 71, 81, 88
religion, 15
rhyme, 19, 33, 38
ritual, elements of, 18
    practice, 71, 82, 140, 170, 189
    questions about, 17
rosemary, 78, 81–82, 89, 99, 103, 111, 140, 145–147, 179, 219

sacred time and space, 18, 78
sage, 111, 211–212
science, 12, 15
secrecy, 19
self-preparation, 6, 63, 71, 81, 93–94, 96, 102, 106–107, 110, 114, 118, 122, 124, 126, 128, 131, 133, 135, 138, 141, 143, 147–148, 151, 157, 160, 164, 166, 169, 171–172, 174, 176–177, 179, 183, 186, 188–190, 192, 195, 198, 201–203, 206, 211, 214, 216, 219–220
sigil, 98, 100
sounds in memory, 38
    in thoughts, 38
St. John's Wort, 179–180
streamlining, ascent to a higher state, 57, 60, 61
    trance induction, 60
success, problems with, 22
sunwise, 77
symbols, 11, 23, 25, 33, 72, 74, 77, 82, 123, 162, 169–173, 175–176, 178, 188–191, 193–197
sympathetic magic, 24, 216

talisman, 98–100
Tetragrammaton, 19
thought form, 192
thoughts, 3, 6, 19, 21, 27, 33, 37–38, 44, 49, 52–53, 55, 65, 76, 94, 97, 107, 129, 138, 141, 143–144, 147–148, 152, 154–155, 183, 192, 194, 199, 204, 210, 213
true nature, defined, 20–21

unconscious mind, defined, 31–33
    function of, 31–33, 36, 47–50, 52, 56, 59, 66, 68, 77, 206–207
unconscious parts, 33–36, 160

widdershins, 77
Will, 4, 6–7, 12–14, 17–24, 27–29, 31–33, 35, 37–39, 44, 47–60, 64–66, 68–89, 93–94, 97–100, 103–108, 110, 112, 119–130, 133–141, 143, 145–152, 156–162, 164, 167–171, 173–175, 177, 179–183, 186–189, 191–217, 219, 221

witness object, 118–119, 122–123, 211–212

words of power, 19, 74, 79–80

yarrow, 98–99, 103–105

LLEWELLYN ORDERING INFORMATION

Order Online:
Visit our website at www.llewellyn.com, select your books, and order them on our secure server.

Order by Phone:
- Call toll-free within the U.S. at 1-877-NEW-WRLD (1-877-639-9753). Call toll-free within Canada at 1-866-NEW-WRLD (1-866-639-9753)
- We accept VISA, MasterCard, and American Express

Order by Mail:
Send the full price of your order (MN residents add 7% sales tax) in U.S. funds, plus postage & handling to:

Llewellyn Worldwide
P.O. Box 64383, Dept. 0-7387-0743-0
St. Paul, MN 55164-0383, U.S.A.

Postage & Handling:

Standard (U.S., Mexico, & Canada). If your order is:
   $49.99 and under, add $3.00
   $50.00 and over, FREE STANDARD SHIPPING

AK, HI, PR: $15.00 for one book plus $1.00 for each additional book.

International Orders (airmail only):
   $16.00 for one book plus $3.00 for each additional book

Orders are processed within 2 business days. Please allow for normal shipping time.
Postage and handling rates subject to change.

Modern Magick
Eleven Lessons in the High Magickal Arts

DONALD MICHAEL KRAIG

Modern Magick is the most comprehensive step-by-step introduction to the art of ceremonial magick ever offered. The eleven lessons in this book will guide you from the easiest of rituals and the construction of your magickal tools through the highest forms of magick: designing your own rituals and doing pathworking. Along the way you will learn the secrets of the Kabbalah in a clear and easy-to-understand manner. You will discover the true secrets of invocation (channeling) and evocation, and the missing information that will finally make the ancient grimoires, such as the "Keys of Solomon," not only comprehensible, but usable. This book also contains one of the most in-depth chapters on sex magick ever written.

   Modern Magick is designed so anyone can use it, and it is the perfect guidebook for students and classes. It will also help to round out the knowledge of long-time practitioners of the magickal arts.

0-87542-324-8
600 pp., 6 x 9, illus. $17.95

"Using Modern Magick"
DONALD MICHAEL KRAIG

The author of *Modern Magick* gives instructions on how to do real magick along with a relaxation exercise and correct pronunciation of magickal words.

0-87542-363-9
audio tape $9.95

To order, call 1-877-NEW-WRLD
Prices subject to change without notice

Postmodern Magic
The Art of Magic in the Information Age

PATRICK DUNN

Fresh ideas for the modern mage lie at the heart of this thought-provoking guide to magic theory. Approaching magical practice from an information paradigm, Patrick Dunn provides a unique and contemporary perspective on an ancient practice.

Imagination, psychology, and authority—the most basic techniques of magic—are introduced first. From there, Dunn teaches all about symbol systems, magical artifacts, sigils, spirits, elementals, languages, and magical journeys, and explains their significance in magical practice. There are also exercises for developing magic skills, along with techniques for creating talismans, glamours, servitors, divination decks, modern defixios, and your own astral temple. Dunn also offers tips on aura detection, divination, occult networking, and conducting your own magic research.

0-7387-0663-9
264 pp., 6 x 9, illus. $14.95

The Magician's Companion
A Practical and Encyclopedic Guide to Magical and Religious Symbolism

BILL WHITCOMB

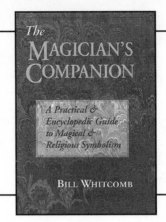

The Magician's Companion is a "desk reference" overflowing with a wide range of occult and esoteric materials absolutely indispensable to anyone engaged in the magickal arts!

The magical knowledge of our ancestors comprises an intricate and elegant technology of the mind and imagination. This book attempts to make the ancient systems accessible, understandable and useful to modern magicians by categorizing and cross-referencing the major magical symbol-systems (i.e., worldviews on inner and outer levels). Students of religion, mysticism, mythology, symbolic art, literature, and even cryptography will find this work of value.

This comprehensive book discusses and compares over thirty-five magical models (e.g., the Trinities, the Taoist Psychic Centers, Enochian magic, the qabala, the Worlds of the Hopi Indians). Also included are discussions of the theory and practice of magic and ritual; sections on alchemy, magical alphabets, talismans, sigils, magical herbs, and plants; suggested programs of study; an extensive glossary and bibliography; and much more.

0-87542-868-1
608 pp., 7 x 10, illus. $24.95

To order, call 1-877-NEW-WRLD
Prices subject to change without notice